13.80

This book will help
you understand and express your
deepest feelings toward others.

Conflict is natural, normal,
neutral, and sometimes even
delightful. It can turn into painful
or disastrous ends, but it doesn't need to.
How we work through our differences,
to a large extent, determines
our whole life pattern. . . .

I am responsible for the way I
react to you. You cannot make me angry
unless I choose to be angry. You cannot make
me discouraged, or disgusted, or depressed.
I am free to react in concerned,
understanding ways. . . .

Love ends the blaming games
and gets on to the real questions:
What is the loving, the responsible, the truly
respectful thing to do now? Where do we go
from here? When do we start?
If not from here—where?
If not now—when?
Who—if not you and me?

Caring enough to Confront

THE LOVE-FIGHT

BY DAVID AUGSBURGER

A Division of G/L Publications
Glendale, California, U.S.A.

The foreign language publishing of all Regal books is under the direction of GLINT. GLINT provides financial and technical help for the adaptation, translation and publishing of books in more than 85 languages for millions of people worldwide.

For more information write: GLINT, 110 W. Broadway, Glendale, CA 91204.

Caring Enough to Confront A Regal Book published by arrangement with Herald Press.

Eleventh Printing, 1979

© Copyright 1973 under the title, *The Love-Fight,* by Herald Press, Scottdale, PA 15683.

Published by
Regal Books Division, G/L Publications
Glendale, California 91209
Printed in U.S.A.

Library of Congress Catalog Card Number 73-83400
ISBN 0-8307-0256-3

Photographs by Paul M. Schrock and Mennonite Broadcasts, Inc.

Contents

Preface

A love-fight? Creative living is care-fronting in conflict?

I touch my fingertips to the underside of your wrist, press, and I'm in touch with the insistent thrust of life pulsating through your whole body.

I listen to your conversation, press past the words to the feelings within, and I'm in touch with the thrusts of your being.

There's the thrust toward being you, becoming all you can be. It drives you to realize the uniqueness of your own self, to move toward the full experience of all the gifts, strengths and abilities that are within you.

There's the thrust toward being free, of separating yourself from others' binding demands or entangled expectations. It presses you toward the joys and the fears of free responsible decision-making.

There's the thrust toward being with others, of experiencing relatedness with others. It draws you to love, to care, to move into trust-commitments, to experience intimacy and community.

I experience these powerful thrusts in me now as I am reaching out to communicate with you. You experience the thrusts of life within you as you weigh and consider what I am saying.

When your thrust as a person runs counter to mine, there is conflict. To deny my own thrust, is to be untrue to the push and the pull of God within me. For me to ignore and do violence to your thrust as a person is to violate your becoming a son of God.

It is not the conflicts that need to concern us, but how the conflicts are handled. The frontal impact of our coming together can be creative, strengthening, and growth producing.

If, that is, we do not choose the cold hostilities of rejection, insult, and affront. Or an incisive but disinterested stance to confront. If we discover care-fronting ways of giving both truth and love, of "truthing it" in love.

It is this dual concern for both integrity and sensitivity in relationships which runs throughout this proposal of the love-fight as a creative way toward expressing both caring and confronting in the conflicts of living with others.

I am indebted most to Dr. Frank W. Kimper for his constant demonstration of love—seeing the preciousness of self-and-other, and of truth—being the truth in finding each other.

I owe much to Drs. Jan and Myron Chartier, for their skills in conflict management and conciliation. And to the consultants in writing both *The Love-Fight,* and the companion radio series *Choice:* Dr.

Roy Umble, Dr. Dan Heinrichs, Jim Gaede, Ernie Isaacs, Kenneth J. Weaver, Waldo Neufeld, James Fairfield, and Matt Meyer.

I have experienced their thrusts in the writing and in the living of the love-fight.

Spring 1973   David Augsburger

1

Care-fronting: The Creative Way Through Conflict

i love you.

if i love you
i must tell you
the truth.

i want your love.

i want your truth.

love me enough to
tell me the truth.

"That was a tasteless thing to do, just like your mother . . ." your husband mutters over dinner. You freeze into angry silence, swallow twice at food gone flat, get up from the table. (Here we go again. He cuts. You retreat to lick the wound.)

You see in his eyes he knows your next move—retreat to the bedroom, an evening-and-night of cold, withdrawn anger. When you feel rejected, you reject. (So? He cuts you off, off you go to sulk.)

"What's the point in running?" you ask yourself. "The longer I brood, the more I hurt. One of these times I'll tell him just how I feel." (Good! Say what you feel, say what you want, say where you are!)

You know now is the time. Then feelings rush out. "When you criticize me like that, I feel rejected. I hurt. I usually run. But what I really want is to feel close to you. And I want your respect." He's looking surprised. He's not used to hearing you admit your feelings, or say what you really want.

When you're cut off by another's sharp words, silent withdrawal is self-defeating. Put out your feelings and get in touch again. Confront by saying what you really want. Care enough to say what you really feel.

* * *

Care-fronting is the key to effective relationships. It's the way to communicate with impact and respect, with truth and love.

"Speaking the truth in love" . . . is *the way* to the mature right relationships shown us in Jesus.

"Truthing-it-in-love," the original phrase St. Paul chose, sums up the caring-confronting way of responding and respecting each other by taking the Jesus way *through* conflict.

Care-fronting has a unique view of conflict. Conflict is natural, normal, neutral, and sometimes even delightful. It can turn into painful or disastrous ends, but it doesn't need to. Conflict is neither good nor bad, right nor wrong. Conflict simply is. How we view, approach and work through our differences does—to a large extent—determine our whole life pattern.

If I view conflict as a fixed matter of fate, explaining, "We just can't get along—we're incompatible—we'll never understand each other—that's all there is to it," then my life pattern will be one of avoiding threat and going my own safe, secure, well-armored way.

If I see conflict as crushing, "If we clash, I'll be judged—I'll be rejected—our friendship will fall

3

through," then my life pattern will be acting the
guy, quickly giving in to keep things comfortable

If I view conflict as an inevitable matter of
and wrong, "I owe it to you, to me, to others, to
to defend my truth and show you your error," m
will be rigid, perhaps perfectionistic, and judgme

If I see conflict as natural, neutral, normal, I
be able to see the difficulties we experience as
sions in relationships and honest differences in
spective that can be worked through by caring a
each other and each confronting the other with
expressed by love.

* * *

Sure you love your husband, most of the time
when he gives you that silent, indifferent treatr
you get all pushed out of shape with anger, anc
never want to see him again, sleep with him a
even hear of him again.

Just when you've chosen the appropriate w
"What a despicable pig you are," you find yo
wondering, "Is that what I really want? To a
him as a person? To hurt him terribly? To utter
ject him?"

Or is it his behavior you want to refuse? If t
it, you don't need to attack him. You can just
front him with how you feel about his silent t
ment, and tell him what you want.

"I want you to hear me," you can say. "I wan
to stay in touch. I want to know what you're fe
too."

4

Caring	Confronting
I care about our relationship.	I feel deeply about the issue at stake.
I want to hear your view.	I want to clearly express mine.
I want to respect your insights.	I want respect for mine.
I trust you to be able to handle my honest feelings.	I want you to trust me with yours.
I promise to stay with the discussion until we've reached an understanding.	I want you to keep working with me until we've reached a new understanding.
I will not trick, pressure, manipulate, or distort the differences.	I want your unpressured, clear, honest view of our differences.
I give you my loving, honest respect.	I want your caring-confronting response.

* * *

"He's stealing me blind," you say, numb with surprise. "Over two hundred dollars must have come in across the counter today, and his cash register ticket shows one hundred twenty-four, seventy-five."

"Of all the stupid blunders, going into a partnership with my brother-in-law has got to be the all-time winner," you say in anger. Opening your pharmacy together had seemed so logical, so right. But in the first nine months you've barely turned a profit.

"The rat. He's been pocketing the cash, ringing up

no-sales, or avoiding the register altogether."
ever the system, he's picking you clean.

"I'll get him. I'll fix his wagon good, the
zler." (Oh, but you can't. It'll hurt your siste
than him, and she's just pulling away from a l
pression.)

"I'll shut up and get out. He can buy my h
have the whole thing—debt, mortgage and all
in his inadequate lap." (Not so easy. Your ho
mortgaged too for the operating capital. You'
the way. To get out, you'll have to let him kn
know.)

"I'll give in and just go along with him for
not say a thing, just stick so close he'll have
fair." (But breathing down his neck as you pe
his shoulder is no solution. You can't be there
time.)

"I've got to confront him with the goods.
no other way out of the mess. But how do I do

* * *

The options: (1) I'll get him, (2) I'll get
I'll give in, (4) I'll meet you halfway, or (5)
enough to confront, are the basic alternatives
most conflict situations.

1. "I'll get him . . ." is the I-win-you-l
cause-I'm-right-you're-wrong position in c
From this viewpoint, the attitude toward co
that the issues are all quite clear—and simple.
one is right—totally right, and someone is w
completely wrong. Fortunately, I'm right (as
and you're wrong. (Except, in this case, it n

6

be the brother-in-law who has his hand in the till after all.)

Obviously, this position is a bit dogmatic, judgmental, and self-righteous. "I have the truth—all the truth—on my side. It's my duty to put you right."

2. "I'll get out . . ." is the I'm-uncomfortable-so-I'll-withdraw stance toward conflict. The viewpoint here is that conflicts are hopeless, people cannot be changed; we either overlook them or withdraw. Conflicts are to be avoided at all costs. When they threaten, get out of their way.

Withdrawal has its advantages, if instant safety is the all-important thing. But it is a way out of conflict, not a way through. And a way out is no way at all.

3. "I'll give in . . ." is the I'll-yield-to-be-nice-since-I-need-your-friendship approach. This perspective on conflict says that differences are disastrous. If they come out into the open, anything can happen. Anything evil, that is. It's far better to be nice, to submit, to go along with the other's demands and stay friends.

Yielding to keep contact will serve you well in many situations. But as a rule, it falls short. You become a doormat. A nice guy. Frustrated. Yet smiling. The more tense and tight on the inside, the more generous and submissive on the outside.

4. "I'll meet you halfway . . ." is the I-have-only-half-the-truth-and-I-need-your-half position. The attitude is one of creative compromise. Conflict is natural, and everyone should be willing to come part way in an attempt to resolve things. A willingness to

give a little will lead to a working solution which is satisfactory to everyone.

Compromise is a gift to human relationships. We move forward on the basis of thoughtful, careful consensus and compromise in most decisions in conflict. But it calls for at least a partial sacrifice of deeply held views and goals which may cost all of us the loss of the best to reach the good of agreement.

5. "I care enough to confront . . ." is the I-want-relationship-and-I-also-want-honest-integrity position. Conflict is viewed as neutral (neither good nor bad) and natural (neither to be avoided nor short-circuited). Working through differences by giving clear messages of "I care" and "I want," which both care and confront, is most helpful.

This is interpersonal communication at its best. Caring—I want to stay in respectful relationships with you, *and* I want you to know where I stand and what I'm feeling, needing, valuing and wanting.

* * *

When that cocksure brother of yours not only insists on proving that he's right, but demands you admit you are wrong (Option one: he wins—you lose), you see instant red. You tense up, ready to go for any remembered weak spot with dagger words. (Option one in reply: you win—he loses.)

You've just found the perfect line to silence him for the rest of the evening, when you stall. "If I stab him with an angry slur, I may be one up on him for the evening, but we'll be farther apart than ever before. What I really want is the guy's respect, not his fear, or his hate." (Considering option five: care and confront, but. . . .)

"Hey, Joe," you say, "you want me to admit I'm wrong? Okay. This round is yours." (Using option three.) "I get up and put you down, then you're up putting me down. Maybe sometimes we're both only half right?" (What about option four?) He's looking tense. Maybe he's scared by your honesty. You give him a grin. He nods a half smile in return. . . . (Maybe you could do option five after all.)

* * *

Seesaw conflicts—when one person tries for a successful I-win-and-you-lose, I'm-up-and-you're-down position—demand that the other reply with an I'll-yield-to-be-nice, I'm-down-and-you're-up stance. Such complementary pairs are so common that many of us learn this approach to working through conflict before all others.

Both the hard-nose boss and the nice-guy employee probably had their styles of getting along with others modeled for them by their parents.

The rigid, demanding, authoritarian father is complemented by the sweet, retiring, submissive wife (who works out her own methods of internalizing her anger, and taking it out on her husband in hidden ways where he doesn't know how to stop her or get back at her).

The critical, nagging, irritable wife is well paired to a silent, withdrawn, passive husband. (He bottles his resentments and strikes back in subtle ways until

that is blocked, then sometimes explodes in ange
an affair.)

*   *   *

It's the end of a usual evening. You're stretc
out in your favorite chair, when your wife pulls
beside you, pad and pencil in hand.

"May I read you the collected sayings of Ch
man You-know-who from the moment you got he
until now?"

"Yeah, if it's all that good," you say.

"Okay. 5:35, 'Hi, I'm home.' 6:20, 'Hambur
again? That all we can afford?' 7:14, 'How come
paper's wet?' 8:03, 'Switch the channel. That'
lousy show.' "

"Look," you say, "you wanted talk? Why did
you marry Hubert Humphrey?"

"All I want is a little companionship," she sa
"You walk in the door, say 'Hi,' then take a vow
silence."

"No, you missed something," you reply. "I w
in, say 'Hi.' You give me that I'm-burned-up-th
you're-late-again look and I know that silence is
only safety, so I shut up. That's why I withdraw."

"You've got it just backwards," she respon
"You withdraw, and the only way I can get any
sponse out of you is to do a little prodding."

That's when it hits you. The two of you are say
the same thing. But each is saying the other starts
Maybe it's one continuous cycle. I nag, you w
draw, I nag, you withdraw, I nag, you withdraw.

"Honey," you say, "who cares which came firs

10

your prodding or my silence. We're stuck in this cycle. How can we break it?"

"I guess I could say something warm instead of digging at you."

"Okay, and I'll say what I really want instead of withdrawing."

* * *

Of the five options in conflict situations—(1) I win—you lose, (2) I want out, I'll withdraw, (3) I'll give in for good relations, (4) I'll meet you halfway, (5) I can care and confront—the last is the most effective, the most truly loving, the most growth-promoting for human relationships.

But all five have their rightful place, their proper time for usage, their appropriate moment.

When another comes on all "I win—you lose," it is appropriate to respond with an "I'll give in for good relations" until the immediate storm is past. Then you can move back to a "I can care and confront" discussion.

When another responds immediately with an "I want out—I withdraw" attitude, again I give in, for good relations can be appropriate for the moment to affirm your deep interest in continuing friendship.

But moving back to care-confront openness as soon as possible is important to you both.

Jesus was free to use any of the five at the appropriate time, place, or conflict.

When the less-than-friendly hometown people of Nazareth rejected His message of confronting love, He chose to withdraw (Luke 4:14-30). He cut off conversation and debate with the Pharisees when the point of clear rejection had arrived (John 11:45-57).

Jesus was also free to act in an "I win—you lose" manner when this was the way to clearest understanding. He confronted the hucksters and hustlers in the temple on win-lose terms (Mark 11:11-19). Or read His clear statements to the religious leaders in Matthew 23.

At His arrest, during His interrogation, throughout His trial, in His unjust beating, and even through His execution, Jesus chose to submit to the anger of others, absorb it, and speak back the word of forgiveness, grace, and acceptance.

But no one has cared—and confronted—with greater effectiveness or more simple clarity than did Jesus.

To the would-be executioners of an accused adulteress, Jesus listened, waiting to hear their persistent questioning, to record all charges in the dust. *Caring.* Then He said, "Let the one among you who has never sinned throw the first stone at her." *Confrontation.*

To the woman, He said, "Where are they all—did no one condemn you?" "No one, sir." "Neither do I condemn you." *Warm, understandable care.* "Go home and do not sin again." *Clear, unmistakable confrontation.* (John 8:7,10,11, *Phillips.*)

To the rich, vain, conceited young ruler, Jesus listened, responded clearly, then looked at him and loved him. He saw that he was loved. Then Jesus confronted. "Go, sell all, give to the poor; and come follow me." Clear enough. (See Mark 10.)

To Nicodemus (John 3), to the outcast minority-group woman at the public watering place (John 4), to the mayor of Capernaum whose son is at the point of death (John 4)—so the account begins. Jesus cared and confronted. He spoke the truth in love. He was truth. He was love.

Truth with love brings healing.

Truth told in love enables men to grow.

Truth in love produces change.

Truth and love are the two necessary ingredients for any relationship with integrity. Love—because all positive relationships begin with friendship, appreciation, respect. And truth—because no relationship of trust can long grow from dishonesty, deceit, betrayal; it springs up from the solid stuff of integrity.

"Confrontation plus caring brings growth just as judgment plus grace brings salvation," Dr. Howard Clinebell, Jr., a favorite teacher of mine, often says.

These are the two arms of genuine relationship: Confrontation with truth. Affirmation with love.

I grow most rapidly when a brother supports me with the arm of loving respect, then confronts me with the arm of clear honesty. Confronting and caring bring growth. Confrontation plus acceptance equals growth.

This is how God relates to us. When we speak of God's relationship with man we have historically used other words.

Judgment and grace lead to salvation.

God's judgment—His radical honesty about truth—confronts us with the demands of disciplined maturity.

God's grace—His undeserved love—reaches out to accept and affirm us at the point we know ourselves to be unacceptable.

Judgment cuts, even kills. If He dealt with us only in judgment, who could stand before Him? If He reached out to us only in love, it would be a cheap grace without integrity. Mere divine permissiveness. Anything goes as far as heaven is concerned. Not so!

Judgment blended with grace.

Confrontation matched with caring.

Truth spoken in love.

Honesty, truth, trust, and love. These all interlock and intertwine in the biblical statements on relationships.

"Love in all sincerity. . . . Care as much about each other as about yourselves" (Romans 12:9,16, *NEB*).

"Love keeps no score of wrongs; does not gloat over other men's sins, but delights in the truth. There is nothing love cannot face; there is no limit to its faith, its hope, and its endurance" (1 Corinthians 13:5-7, *NEB*).

" 'Love your neighbor as yourself.' But if you go on fighting one another, tooth and nail, all you can expect is mutual destruction" (Galatians 5:14,15, *NEB*).

"No, let us speak the truth in love; so shall we fully grow up into Christ. . . . Bonded and knit together by every constituent joint, the whole frame grows through the due activity of each part, and builds itself up in love" (Ephesians 4:15,16, *NEB*).

For Further Experience

1.   Do a mental rehearsal of both caring and confronting in conflicts you experienced today, or anticipate tomorrow. Place the other person in a chair in front of you and hold out your left hand saying, "I do care, I want to respect you, I want your respect." Alternate by reaching out with the right hand to say, "But I want you to know how I feel. I want to tell you where I am. I have this goal in our relationship." Work both sides of yourself. Become aware of which is more difficult. In which are you least practiced. Stay with it until feelings of caring and statements of goal both come clear.

2. Check back through your relationships of the past week. Fill in appropriate situations.

(1) I win, you lose stance _____

_____

(2) I want out, I withdraw attitude _____

_____

(3) I'll give in for good relations _____

_____

(4) I'll meet you halfway _____

_____

(5) I can care and confront _____

_____

Which was effective? Which was most comfortable? Which was used most frequently? Which do you want to use more often?

2

Truthing It:
A Simplified
Speech Style

I want to
hear you,
feel what you feel.
I want to speak clearly
simply with word-windows
that let you see
all the way in
to where I live
laugh
and
cry.

"It's been months since I really talked with my husband; we've grown so far apart," you say in numb realization. "He has his life. I have mine. We see each other but we don't meet."

Your husband's job demands long hours. He hasn't time to hear you. Your job takes a lot of you. You're too tired to reach out to him. Now the constant thing in your marriage is conflicts.

"Five years have gone by without much conversation," you say. "We need to reshuffle our cards and deal each other a new hand. I think I'll suggest that tonight, suggest we try to find out what each of us expects from the other now. We're going to be home tonight for a change. If I can just listen well enough that he can start talking. Maybe if I ask about his needs, find out what he's wanting from me first, then we could hear each other without fighting."

A relationship is only as good as its communication. Take time—enough time—to hear what the other needs and wants. You can cancel a lot of old expectations and choose some new ones—on a fifty-fifty basis—giving each partner equal opportunities at life, equal freedom to choose, equal chance to express herself or himself.

* * *

"It is certain that a relationship will be only as good as its communication. If you and I can honestly tell each other who we are, that is, what we think, judge, feel, value, love, honor and esteem, hate, fear, desire, hope for, believe in and are committed to, then and then only can each of us grow. Then and then alone can each of us be what he really is, say what he really thinks, tell what he really feels, express what he really loves. This is the real meaning of authenticity as a person, that my exterior truly reflects my interior. It means I can be honest in the communication of my person to others. And this I cannot do unless you help me. Unless you help me, I cannot grow, or be happy, or really come alive.

"I have to be free and able to say my thoughts to you, to tell you about my judgments and values, to expose to you my fears and frustrations, to admit to you my failures and shames, to share my triumphs, before I can really be sure what it is that I am and can become. I must be able to tell you who I am before I can know who I am. And I must know who I am before I can act truly, that is, in accordance with my true self."[1]

* * *

You park on the street, wanting her not to hear
car tires in the driveway. You cross the lawn and
yourself in by the French doors to the dining room

It's midafternoon. Work caught up. Good time
a round of golf. None of the guys are free. It's b
so long since you've done anything fun with y
wife, you decide to make up by making it a twoso
Now here you are, stepping burglar-like toward
family room.

The sound of voices stops you. You stand fro
in half-stride hearing your wife talking in an intim
tone that seems from long ago.

"Why don't you tell your husband how you fe
the other woman is asking. You recognize
friend's voice.

"There's no point in it," she replies. "He woul
hear me anyway."

"Don't you talk about things that are close to yc

"Talk? Small talk. That's all it is. But he doe
really hear me. If he knows at all what I think,
certainly doesn't understand how I feel."

"Can't you tell him?"

"No," she says. "There's no point in trying.
lives on superficial friendships. Even with me. I
hardly acquainted with the kids. And me? He doe
listen. Sometimes I get so lonely I could. . . ."

You turn, tiptoeing toward the door.

You're hearing, for a change, you admit to yo
self.

Do you want to hear? Do you want to talk v
her? Do you want to break into relationship?

22

When I listen:

I want to hear you. To hear deeply. Truthing it in communication is truly hearing what another says, how it is said, and what feeling is conveyed. To hear with an inner ear is to tune in to the feelings, the hurts, the angers, the demands of another.

I want to hear you, and not hear myself interpreting you. I am aware of two strong tendencies: (1) to "read in" things I feel as I listen and miss what you are wanting to tell me; and (2) to "read out" and totally miss what I don't want to hear from you because it threatens, confronts, rejects, ignores me and my viewpoint.

I want to hear you accurately, so I'll need to check out what I hear at crucial points to be as sure as I can that my meanings match your meanings. I get an inkling of what your meanings are from your words, your tone of voice, your face, gestures, and body movements. But it is only an inkling. I must check it out at times by replaying what I heard for your approval, until you agree that you have been heard.

I want to hear deeply, clearly, accurately enough that I am able—to some real extent—to feel what you feel, hurt a bit where you hurt, and want for you the freedom to be all you are becoming.

* * *

"It's okay, Honey, no problem," you say to your husband on the phone. It's the fourth night in a row he's chosen to work late, and called you with last-minute apologies. It's not really okay with you, even though you keep saying it is. But that's always been your style. Be agreeable, give in to others, say everything's okay, bottle your feelings until finally you explode over some stupidly simple thing and say things you hate as soon as you hear them.

Always giving in is no good. Accumulating grievances is even less helpful. Dishonest statements to cover it all is even worse. And when the anger eruption comes, it's totally ineffectual.

"I've got to start dealing with things as they come up, not just postpone my feelings and let them simmer," you say. "Like that phone call right now. I could have said, 'No, it's not okay. I have special things planned. I am irritated at your being out the last three nights. I want to be with you tonight.' I could have said it straight and simply."

What stops you from leveling like that? You stop yourself. "It's not too late," you tell yourself. "I can still ring him back." You pick up the phone and begin dialing. I'll say, "I want to be with you tonight. Try to change things. Come home on time. . . ."

Keep short books with your feelings. Stay up-to-date. Find ways of reporting feelings as they occur. Experiment in saying both what you feel and what you really want. "I do care about you. I want to be close. I want more time together. I need to tell you when I'm angry. Love me enough to listen to me."

* * *

When I speak:
I want to speak simply. To say what I mean in the

clearest, shortest, frankest words I know. I want to reach out with my meanings to meet your meanings. (Communication is a meeting of meaning.) Knowing that meanings are in people, not in words, I want to be as clear and open about my meanings as I can. (Words don't mean. People mean.)

I want to speak personally. I speak from my experience. So I want to say, "I think . . ." "I feel . . ." instead of, "People think . . ." or "You get the feeling . . ." To declare my personal feelings and convictions calls for courage. It is more risky than saying, "Most people, it seems, sometimes feel, to some extent . . ."

I want to speak for myself, not for others. I will not say, "I think you think that I think . . ." I will not try to second-guess your feelings, thoughts, attitudes. I do not care to speak for you. I want to listen as you speak to me, and respond.

I want to speak honestly. Truthing it is trusting others with my actual feelings and viewpoints. Avoiding honest statements of real feelings and viewpoints is often considered kindness, thoughtfulness, or generosity. More often it is the most cruel thing I can do to others. It is a kind of benevolent lying.

Selective honesty is not honesty at all. I find myself using it (1) to avoid real relationships with others when I'm too rushed or bushed to give them my time; (2) to avoid clear confrontations with others; (3) to manipulate situations or facts to protect myself or others. I don't like such defense systems, no matter how comfortable they may seem. I want to be truthful in all situations. I want to pay others the compliment of believing they can handle honest feelings. I want to put out what I feel, where I am, how think.

I want to speak directly. I do not want to ta about people when it is possible to talk to ther Whatever I have to say to you, I want you to he first from me.

I want to give statements instead of asking que tions. Some questions are simple requests for clari cation, or further information. But many questio are double-talk. They are ways of making comment criticisms, or attacks while avoiding the full respon bility for what is said. They are ways of giving mul level messages that leave the listener with a multip choice test with every question.

Take the simple response, "What do you mean that?" It can mean (1) Will you tell me your mea ing again? (2) What are you implying about m (3) How dare you say that to me? (4) You're tacking me. It has as many levels as the hearer m choose. And the hearer must choose. But no matt which meaning he chooses to answer, the question can say, "You misunderstand."

"Why" questions are even more effective as a w of manipulating others. I want to eliminate the wo "why" from my relationships.

* * *

"Why do you always leave your things lying over the house?" you ask.

"Why can't you pick up after yourselves?"

"Why don't you show a little interest in things?"

26

No one answers you. It's like your questions go unheard.

"Why can't I get a little cooperation?"

Your son looks up at you. "Why does everything you say begin with the word 'why'?" he asks.

"Why shouldn't it?" you snap.

"I don't know," he says, "but it feels like a trap. If we say why, you can shout us down, say our reasons are no good."

"What do you want me to say?" you ask. (First question without a "why.")

"Just tell us what you want," he replies. "Like I'm doing to you now. Don't bear-trap us. Just be honest with us."

Most of us can do with a lot fewer questions. Especially those beginning with "why."

We use questions to give hidden messages of anger. Anger we are unwilling to own honestly.

We use questions to hit and run. You can cut with a question and then deny that you meant it to hurt the other.

Love gives up the concealed weapons called questions, and makes clear statements like: I care about you. I need you. I want your help. I want your respect. Love is honestly open in conversation. Love sets no traps.

*   *   *

I want to negotiate differences with others in clear, respectful, truthful ways of speaking and acting. I want conflict to call out the best in myself and others. I want both the truth as I see it, and respect for the other to be clear in my responses, verbal and nonverbal.

When situations of conflict become difficult, I want to speak clearly, honestly, personally, directly, in simple statements. This provides the greatest impact with the least confusion or distortion. I may or may not be able to break through the conflict to understanding, but I can express both love and truth best by refusing the "whys" and the "it's your fault's."

* * *

"Why did you take the car last night when you knew I'd be needing it?" your husband says to your son—to your son's indifferent back. He shrugs his shoulders as a reply. "I want to know why you deliberately defy me."

"Man, I'm just doing my thing," you son replies. "You're free to do yours."

They're talking past each other again. Do you want to intervene? "I want to know why you try to spite me," your husband is saying. The boy's ignoring him. To answer is to walk into a bear trap. If he says "Why?" his dad will say, "That's stupid." It's like a cycle of move and countermove that you do your best to avoid.

"Count me out of their fights," you say. But maybe you could referee. Get them to agree to some simple ground rules. Maybe they could learn to fight a little more fairly?

A few simple guidelines for cleaning up fights are: the person who has a complaint should make the first move to discuss it; one complaint to a session; no trapping questions, just clear statements. Try giving honest, clean "beefs" (sharply pointed complaints or criticisms) like, "The behavior you do is . . . When you do it I feel . . . What I really want is . . ." Have the other repeat the beef. Then respond with a clear yes, no, or compromise offer.

Simple rules—but they're the way of truthing it in love through conflict.

* * *

Clear communication is giving clean, simple "yes" and "no" responses.

"Whatever you have to say," Jesus counseled, "let your 'yes' be a plain 'yes' and your 'no' be a plain 'no'—anything more than this has a taint of evil" (Matthew 5:37, *Phillips*).

"Now it is a matter of pride to us—endorsed by our conscience—that. . . . our dealings with you have been absolutely aboveboard and sincere before God," St. Paul once wrote. "Our words have no double meaning—they mean just what you understand them to mean when you read them. I do not speak with my tongue in my cheek, saying 'yes' and meaning 'no,' . . . saying one thing and meaning another" (2 Corinthians 1:12,13,18,22, paraphrased from *Phillips*).

Love is giving clear "yes's and no's."

* * *

"Sure, count me in. I'll be glad to help out," you

say into telephone receiver, "I like working w
boys. Coaching Little League sounds fun. Right,
be at the meeting." You turn from the phone to
your wife's questioning eyes.

"It's just Monday and Thursday nights," you
plain. "It's important for the community. I can't
no."

"If we had a boy in Little League, it'd be
ferent," your wife says. "But, Joe, you don't have
time."

"I can make time for it," you say. "I just can't
no to things that oughta be done."

"But when you accept that," your wife rep
"you're saying no to having time with me and
girls, you're saying no to having time for yourself.

"Yeah, you're right. I've already got the club
Thursdays, night school Wednesdays, bowling
Fridays, not to mention all the extras."

"When do you start saying no?" your wife a
"With no time together, we're becoming strang
and what time we have we spend fighting."

"I can't say no," you begin again.

"Won't say 'no,' " your wife corrects.

"Yeah, that's it. I'm afraid they'll quit asking
in on things if I cut out once. I don't want t
passed by. But I want time with my family
Maybe I can say no. I think I will."

You can say no—if you will. You can say n
you've first said a bigger yes to time for your fa
time for close relationships, time to be humans
gether.

Say yes to your family. Guard that yes with
calendar.

Live that yes by being close.

* * *

When I decide:
I want to give clear "yes-signals" or "no-signals."
Yes signals come easy. No signals often come hard.
"No" is one of the hardest words to pronounce—
face to face.

"I can't say no to the boss," a young man tried to
explain to me last night. "I've got to do what he asks.
It's the only way open to me. I have no choice." I
doubt it.

"I can't say no to Ted, I just can't." The young
wife who gave that excuse for her indecision over a
growing friendship with her employer, can't say no
because she won't say no.

To say "I can't" is seldom true. More often it's a
way of avoiding responsibility for making a decision.
"I won't say no," would be more accurate. "I refuse
to take responsibility for myself and say no."

* * *

You feel the stiffness around your mouth as you
walk away from the boss. You know you must have
had your perma-smile pasted on. Funny, you weren't
smiling inside. Now you're going to rush through
lunch so you can run an errand for the guy at the
next bench. "No bother at all," you insisted. But it
is . . .

"I'm a nice guy," you say to yourself. "I'm just too
nice to people. I smile, I say yes—yes—yes, and yet

inside I feel tired. I wish they'd lean on somebody else for a change. When they ask for something, I say, 'Anything for a friend.' If they impose, I say, 'What's a friend for?' If they get angry, I say, 'Come on, let's be friends.'

"I'm an insufferably nice guy. Except inside. There I'm like anybody else. What I'd like is to be able to say no. What I want is to be free to choose when I'd like to be honest with people, to really be me."

Always being Mr. Nice-Guy, and then turning your real feelings into stomach acid is self-defeating. You may get what you want—for the moment—by lathering others, but you don't like yourself for it.

Consider putting out what you're feeling in simple honesty. As Jesus put it, "Let your yes be a clear yes, and your no, no. Anything else spells trouble."

* * *

"Not to decide is to decide," theologian Harvey Cox is quoted on posters and subway walls.

Not to decide is to decide—to decide for the status quo, to decide for the state you now are in, to decide to stay stuck, to choose to stay in the circular trap of irresponsibility.

"I can't make up my mind, I can't decide, so I refuse to consider the alternatives. I shift the responsibility on others. I wait for circumstances to change, so I won't need to choose since I can't make up my mind." Full circle. Vicious circle. Endless circle.

Or as another friend put it for me last week, "I just can't hurt my girl friend by telling her the painful truth, so I postpone honesty. I put off the terrible day. I'm hurting her more all the time because I just can't bring myself to hurt her by telling the truth." Full circle. Irresponsible circle.

Not to decide is to decide for irresponsibility.

To say "I can't decide," is to decide for what you really may not want.

To say "I can't decide," is to nurture the false fantasy that my life is controlled by fate. The script for such a life-style goes like this:

I had no choice in my birth.
I didn't pick my parents.
I was messed up in childhood.
I grew up in a vise. I couldn't move.
I had no say about anything.
I had to stay in line, no back talk.
By the time I was a teen-ager, it was all decided. I
     was all determined.
I never had a chance.
Not enough money.
Not the right family.
Not a good education.
Not one chance to change it.
Not a single opportunity to be different.
It's all in the stars/cards/genes/fates.
I live with all the wrong breaks, no luck.
I'll die when my number comes up, and that's that.
I never had a chance.
I've no choice.
I can't help it.
Can't say yes.
Can't say no.
Poor me.

Nonsense. You and I are decisional beings. We are free to choose. We have the right to choose. We are responsible for our choices—to choose or not to choose.

God Himself has gifted us with this responsibility. He gave us this "response-ability," this ability to respond to life. We have the ability to respond to whatever situations come to us, in a decisional, if not a decisive, way.

We can say no. The ability to say a clear yes and a clear no is the key to responsible freedom in living.

Jesus had an unusual way of dealing with people who were stuck between yes and no.

A wealthy young man came asking for one extra act which would end his dissatisfaction with himself. "Nothing doing," Jesus replied. "You can do better than that. You're stuck with all your wealth. Break loose and live. You can choose to use it, not be used by it. You can be free from its bondage."

"I can't," the man replied with his back as he turned silently away.

"He won't," Jesus corrected. To give up wealth is hard, but it's possible.

Men may say, "I can't." With them it seems impossible. God says, "You can, but you won't." Everything is possible with God. (See Mark 10:17-27.)

Say no. Or yes. With clear, simple, honest, statements of truth given in love.

For Further Experience

1. Practice listening skills to learn new ways of hearing, feeling with, caring for others.

(1) Sit at eye level with a child. Let your own

34

inner child come out and play with the little boy or girl who is talking to you. Listen with your eyes. Check out what you're hearing. Find some way to affirm his or her preciousness.

(2) Listen to a friend. Communicate love without putting it in words. Avoid asking any questions, prompting or completing his sentences.

(3) Listen to someone you rather dislike. Try to really hear him or her, for a change. Become aware of your own resistances to getting close. Extend some word of understanding, appreciation, or simple joy.

(4) Listen to God. With pencil in hand. Take notes on new awarenesses. Let your mind flow freely, but keep things open by being aware that He is communicating love to you.

2. Practice simple, clear, single-level speech.

(1) Drop all exaggeration or additional coloring of language for effect; use fewer adjectives.

(2) Refuse all pretenses—of knowing things you only guess, of being better informed or more certain of facts than you are.

(3) Live for a day without questions. If you need information, say "I'm wondering if . . ." or "I'm wanting to know . . ."

(4) Find fresh clear ways of saying yes and no without dishonesty. Instead of "I'm sorry but I can't," try "No, thank you. I'm wanting that time for my family."

---

1. John Powell, *Why Am I Afraid to Tell You Who I Am?* (Los Angeles: Argus Communications, 1969).

3
Owning Anger:
Let Both
Your Faces Show

I AM NOT ANGRY!
(I'M JUST CONCERNED.)

I DON'T GET ANGRY!
(I JUST FEEL HURT.)

SEE? YOU MADE ME ANGRY!
(IT'S ALL YOUR FAULT.)

YOU BURN ME UP!
(IT'S YOU IN THE WRONG.)

You're standing in the living room, looking out the window at your son's back. You're replaying the last moment's conversation. "How stupid can you get?" you'd said. "You blew it again like a no-good kid. That's what you are, and you better shape up or you're shipping out."

There he goes, anger and rejection showing in the slump of his shoulders. "He blew it?" you ask yourself. "Well, I blew it even worse. I get angry, I attack him personally, I put him down, I chop away at his self-esteem. I'm getting nowhere. What else can we do? If I could just deal with what he's doing without attacking him. Maybe that would make a difference. I could try it."

When angry, are you likely to attack the other person, depreciating his personality, intelligence, skill, or worth? It doesn't get you what you want either, I'll bet.

40

Next time, try focusing your anger on the person's behavior. Express appreciation for the other as a person, even as you explain your anger at his or her way of behaving. It lets you stay in touch while getting at what you are angry about. And, as Jesus demonstrated, you can be both angry (at behaviors) and loving (toward persons) at the same time.

*　*　*

Do you feel comfortable with the suggestion that anger is acceptable, that it can be openly owned, that anger is a normal, natural human emotion?

Dr. Ernest Bruder, an outstanding chaplain and counselor, writes, "Growing angry is a quite normal (though very bothersome) response in human relations, but it does cut the individual off from those who are important to him. For some this is so intolerable that the anger is never admitted to awareness and the individual tries to deny those feelings which are a part of his connection with the rest of humanity."[1]

Anger is not the essence of badness.

Jesus felt free to be angry, to let His anger show, to express His anger clearly, and to feel no apparent misgivings or remorse.

*　*　*

It happened in a place of worship, the synagogue. A handicapped man with paralysis of the hand came asking for healing.

The religious leaders are (1) looking on with malice, (2) anticipating that Jesus may break their ceremonial blue laws against doing a service for another on the Sabbath, (3) hoping for some such infraction of the law so they can charge Him with illegal, irreligious, irresponsible action.

Jesus avoids neither the man in need nor His own critics.

"Stand up and come out here in front," He says to the man.

Open, simple, clear honest action.

Then He turns to the Pharisees. He is aware of their demands—demands characteristic of many religious leaders through the centuries—(1) that principles come before the pain of persons, (2) that religious piety be honored above the needs of a brother, (3) that legalistic obedience is more important than human life and love for others. Jesus focuses their demands in the kind of question-statements they were so fond of debating. But in doing so, He is clearly confronting and refusing their demands.

There is silence. (As an answer, silence is often violence.)

Jesus is deeply hurt at their inhumanity.

He looks at them in anger. His look sweeps from one face to another. His demand is clear. Be human. Be loving. Care about people. Respect this man's needs. See him as precious.

Then Jesus does the responsible, loving, caring thing. "Stretch out your hand," He says to the man.

He stretches it out, and it is as sound as the other. (Mark 3:1-6, paraphrased from *Phillips*.)

That is clear, focused, creative, controlled, dynamic anger.

* * *

Hate is sin	Love is virtue
Anger is evil	Affection is good
Confronting is brutal	Caring is wonderful
Openness is questionable	Diplomacy is wise

Do you find yourself thinking in such clearly defined categories? Rejecting hate, anger, honest awareness, and expression of your true feelings and perspectives and clear confrontation with others? To cut off one-half of your emotional spectrum and reject all negative feelings is to refuse to be a whole person. To deny and repress everything on the negative side is to also stifle and crush the full expression of your positive side.

There is danger in abusing and misusing others with our positive emotions and actions—love, kindness, gentleness, tolerance, sweetness—just as there is the threat of cutting and destroying others with our negative responses—anger, harshness, criticism, irritation. To be engulfed and incorporated by a smothering love, all sweet gentleness, and I'm-only-trying-to-help-you-it's-for-your-own-good kindness is more treacherous than harsh, crisp frankness. You can at least reject it without fighting an affectionate, sticky mass of divinity-candy love.

I want to be a whole person in my relationships with you. I want to be in touch with both sides of you. Give me both your cold pricklies (honest anger) and your warm fuzzies (affirming love). Let both your faces show.

There are two sides in everyone. Both sides are

43

important. Both are acceptable. Both are precious. Both can be loved.

I prefer to think that God wants my very best and only my best. That He'll have nothing to do with my weakness, my timidity, my fears.

Not so. The God I am experiencing right now accepts me—weakness as well as strength, fear as well as confidence, anger as well as gentleness.

He loves the whole me.

He loves the whole you.

His love makes wholeness possible in its most complete form. As I know and experience the love of God, His acceptance reaches out to include both sides of me. "God knows the best and the worst about me," I can say. "And, what do you know? He loves me anyway."

I can be aware of my feelings of anger. (I am accepted.)

I can own my resentments, my hate, my hostility. (I am loved.)

I can discover new ways of experiencing my negative and my positive feelings. (I am free to grow.)

I can be angry in creative, loving, caring ways. (I see it modeled in Jesus.)

* * *

Your wife made a cutting remark two days ago, and still no apology. Your daughter didn't thank you for the little gift you bought her. Your son forgot to put the tools back in their place in your shop. And you're feeling angry at all of them, at everything!

Anger is a demand. Like, "I demand an apology

44

from you—an apology that suits me." "I demand you show appreciation for my gifts—in a way that pleases me." "I demand that you return my tools—perfectly—just the way I keep them." That's the real thrust of anger. A demand that also demands others meet your demands.

Even though you seldom put the demands into words, they are there inside your feelings. And you are resentful. "What if I said what I feel, if I really made my demands clear?" you ask yourself. "Then I could either stick to them, or laugh at them and forget them. . . ."

Get in touch with the demands you make of others. Recognize them. Start admitting them out loud. Then you have a choice: (1) you can negotiate the demands that matter, or (2) you can cancel the ones that don't.

Love is being honest and open about your demands. Love is canceling unfair demands. Love is freeing others to live and grow.

* * *

Underneath my feelings of anger . . .
 . . . there are concealed expectations.
 (I may not yet be aware of them myself.)
Inside my angry statements . . .
 . . . there are hidden demands.
 (I may not yet be able to put them into words.)

Recognized or unrecognized, the demands are there. Anger is a demand. It may be a demand that you hear me. Or that you recognize my worth. Or that you see me as precious and worthy to be loved. Or that you respect me. Or let go of my arm. Or quit trying to take control of my life.

The demands emerge whenever I see you as rejecting me, or foresee you as about to reject me as a person of worth.

Dr. Frank Kimper, a great teacher of pastoral care, writes of this: "You are precious simply because you are. You were born that way. *To see that, and to be grasped by the reality of it, is to love.*

"Experience seems to indicate that harmonious relations are possible *only when that attitude is maintained.* This universal law has been stated in many ways—by the Jews as a simple and direct command of God, 'Thou shalt love thy neighbor as thyself.' The clause, 'as thyself,' correctly implies that *love of self is innate.* Every person senses *instinctively* the priceless nature of his own being, and reacts *reflexively* to preserve it against any threat.

"More specifically, each of us is automatically 'defensive' in the face of perceived rejection. To be ignored as though I did not exist, or to be treated as though I were worthless, is repulsive. Instinctively, spontaneously I react to affirm the priceless nature of my own being by becoming angry and lashing back or, feeling very hurt, by withdrawing within some protective shell to safeguard as best I can the treasured 'me' I know I am.

"But my reaction to being ignored or rejected has also a second purpose: to demand by angry words or pouting that others recognize the preciousness of the self I am, and respond accordingly. Such demands

46

fail because in making my demand I reject and ignore the very persons I want to love me; and once horns are locked in that way, the only solution is for one or the other of us (or both) to adopt an attitude of love—to see and affirm the other to be as precious as I am, *no matter what his performance*.

"I have never met a human being who did not have similar spiritual reflexes. Because to love one's self is a 'built-in reflex.' Each of us was created that way."[2]

* * *

Anger is a demand "that you recognize my worth." When I feel that another person is about to engulf or incorporate me (assuming ownership of me, taking me for granted, using me, absorbing me into his or her life-program), I feel angry.

Actually, I first feel anxious. "Anxiety is a sign that one's self-esteem, one's self-regard is endangered,"[3] as Harry Stack Sullivan expressed it. When my freedom to be me is threatened, I become anxious, tense, ready for some action. Escape? Anger? Or work out an agreement?

Escape may be neither possible nor practical. Agreement seems far away since I see you as ignoring my freedom, devaluing my worth, and attempting to use me. Anger is the most available option.

Anger is "the curse of interpersonal relations," Sullivan well said. A curse, because it is so instantly effective as a way of relieving anxiety. When a person flashes to anger, the anger clouds his recall of what just happened to spark the anger, confuses his awareness of what he is really demanding, and restricts his ability to work toward a new agreement.

But we chose—consciously or unconsciously—to become angry because:

"Anger is much more pleasant to experience than anxiety. The brute facts are that it is much more comfortable to feel angry than anxious. Admitting that neither is too delightful, there is everything in favor of anger. Anger often leaves one sort of worn out . . . and very often makes things worse in the long run, but there is a curious feeling of power when one is angry."[4]

Check the pattern: (1) I feel keen frustration in my relationship with another. (2) I see the other person as rejecting me—my worth, my needs, my freedom, my request. (3) I become suddenly and intensely anxious. (4) I blow away my anxiety with anger which confuses things even further. (5) I may then feel guilty for my behavior and resentful of the other's part in the painful experience.

Anger is a positive emotion, a self-affirming emotion which responds reflexively to the threat of rejection or devaluation with the messages (1) I am a person, a precious person and (2) I demand that you recognize and respect me.

The energies of anger can flow in self-affirming ways when directed by love—the awareness of the other person's equal preciousness.

Anger energies become a creative force when they are employed (1) to change my own behavior which ignored the other's preciousness and (2) to confront

48

the other with his or her need to change unloving behavior. Anger energy can be directed at the cause of the anger, to get at the demands I am making, to own them, and then either correct my demanding self by canceling the demand, or call on the other to hear my demand and respond to how I see our relationship and what I want.

When I am on the receiving end of another's anger, I want to hear the anger-messages the other gives to me, and check out what I am picking up as a demand. Careful listening can discern what the other is demanding, clarify it in clear statements, and lead to clean confrontation. Then I have the choice of saying yes to the other's demands, or saying no. I may feel angry in return, but I want to experience my anger with honest "I statements," not with explosive "you statements."

Explosive anger is "the curse of interpersonal relations." Vented anger may ventilate feelings and provide instant, though temporary, release for tortured emotions, but it does little for relationships.

Clearly expressed anger is something different. Clear statements of anger feelings and angry demands can slice through emotional barriers or communications tangles and establish contact.

When angry, I want to give clear, simple "I messages." "You messages" are most often attacks, criticisms, devaluations of the other person, labels, or ways of fixing blame.

"I messages" are honest, clear, confessional. "I messages" own my anger, my responsibility, my demands without placing blame. Note the contrast between honest confession and distorted rejection.

I messages	You messages
I am angry.	You make me angry.
I feel rejected.	You're judging and rejecting me.
I don't like the wall between us.	You're building a wall between us.
I don't like blaming or being blamed.	You're blaming everything on me.
I want the freedom to say yes or no.	You're trying to run my life.
I want respectful friendship with you again.	You've got to respect me or you're not my friend.

* * *

Harry's been your friend for years. You could always count on him. Now you hurt him. He's turned against you. Last month it was Steve. You cut him off in an angry moment; it hasn't been the same. People you've been close to for years now hold you at a distance. . . .

"So what. If they want to let me down, who needs them," you tell yourself. But inside you say, "I need them. I want their friendship. But I drive them away from me. It's like I've been carrying an overload of anger in my gut.

"I've got to talk it out with someone," you tell yourself. But where do you turn? "I need to talk to someone about who to talk to," you say. "Maybe my minister would listen to me and suggest where I could find out what's bugging me."

When you find yourself carrying a lot of anger

along as extra baggage, talk it out with someone you trust—a friend, your minister, your doctor. And reach out to others for new ways of respectful behaving that you get where you really want to be with your friends.

* * *

"I just can't help it. It makes me angry."

"It just gets to me and touches off my temper."

"It's like something comes over me, and I can't do a thing about it."

"It's other people, that's what it is. They know I've got a quick temper and they're out to get me."

"It" is the problem. "It" causes untold irritation, anger, frustration, embarrassment, pain, guilt, and misery. "It's" not me. "It's" this something, or someone, or some situations.

When you find yourself using "it" as an explanation or as a scapegoat, stop. Listen to yourself. Recognize what you're doing. Avoiding responsibility. Sidestepping the real problem. Denying ownership of your feelings, responses, and actions.

Release comes not from denying, but from owning who—what—and where I am in my relationships.

I want to own what goes on in me and accept total responsibility for it.

I discover that as I own it, accepting full responsibility, I am then able to respond in new ways. I become response-able.

A great freedom comes as I own my thoughts, feelings, words, and emotions. (1) I become free to choose my actions. (2) I become free to choose my reactions.

My actions are mine. Your actions are yours. I am responsible for my behavior. You are responsible for yours.

I also accept responsibility for my actions.

"You make me angry," I used to say.

Untrue. No one can make another angry. If I become angry at you, I am responsible for that reaction. (I am not saying that anger is wrong. It may well be the most appropriate and loving response that I am aware of at that moment.)

But you do not make me angry. I make me angry at you. It is not the only behavior open to me.

There is no situation in which anger is the only possible response. If I become angry (and I may, it's acceptable) it's because I choose to respond with anger. I might have chosen kindness, irritation, humor, or many other alternatives (if I had been aware of these choices). There is no situation which commands us absolutely. For example, I have the choice to respond to another's threat with blind obedience, with silent passivity, with vocal refusal, with firm resistance, or with anger, if that seems appropriate.

When childhood experiences are limited, a person may mature with a limited set of behaviors open to him or her. Some have only two ways of coping with another's attack—anger or submission. If these are the only ways modeled by the parents or the family, they may be the only aware-choices in the person's behavioral repertoire.

If I have grown enough in life so that more than one pattern of behavior is available to me, then I can freely select the responses which seem most appropriate to the situation.

I want to be aware of a wealth of responses, and to have them available to me. Anger or patience. Toughness or gentleness. Clear confrontation or warm, caring support. I want to be able-to-respond in any of these.

I am responsible for choosing my responses to you.

I am responsible for the way I react to you.

I am responsible for how I see you. And from the way I see you—as either friendly or hostile; accepting or rejecting; welcoming or threatening—emerge my feelings. Feelings are the energies that power the way I choose to see you, or to perceive you.

I am responsible for how I see you—and from that for the way I feel about you.

You cannot make me angry. Unless I choose to be angry.

You cannot make me discouraged, or disgusted, or depressed. These are choices.

You cannot make me hate. I must choose to hate.

You cannot make me jealous. I must choose envy.

I experience all these and more on all too many occasions, but I am responsible for those actions or reactions. I make the choice.

And I am free to choose loving responses. I am free to choose trusting replies. I am free to react in concerned, understanding ways if I choose to see the other person as precious, as valuable, as worthy of love because he or she is equally loved of God.

53

*   *   *

I love me.
I love my freedom
   to be who I am.
I love my drive
   to be all I can be.
I love my right
   to be different from you.
I love my need
   to be related to you.

I also love you.
I respect your freedom
   to be who you are.
I admire your drive
   to be all you can be.
I recognize your right
   to be different from me.
I appreciate your need
   to be related to me.

*   *   *

The thoughts I think,
The words I speak,
The actions I take,
The emotions I feel—
   They are mine, for them
   I am fully responsible.

The thoughts you think,
The words you speak,
The actions you take,
The emotions you feel—
   They are yours, for them
   I am in no way responsible

*   *   *

I am free
to accept or to refuse
   your wants
   your requests
   your expectations
   your demands.
I can say yes.
I can say no.
I am not in this world
   to live as you prescribe.

You are free
to accept or to refuse
   my wants
   my requests
   my expectations
   my demands.
You can say yes.
You can say no.
You are not in this world
   to live as I prescribe.

* * *

I am not responsible *for* you.	You are not responsible *for* me.
I will not be responsible *to* you.	You need not be responsible *to* me.
I want to be responsible *with* you.	You can be responsible *with* me.
I want to be your brother.	You may be a brother with me.

For Further Experience

1. Read Psalm 40, and notice David's frank honesty with God as the feelings flow out. List the feelings from depression, to release, to elation, to fear, to joy in helping others, to anger, to resentment, to trust and final impatience.

2. To put your negative feelings into words, and own them as a part of the you God loves, complete the phrases in at least five ways:

"I get angry when . . ."

". . . and my behavior is . . ."

". . . and afterward I feel . . ."

". . . What I really want is . . ."

3. To get in touch with the demands inside your anger, end this sentence in five ways:

"When I become angry, my demands are . . ."

4. To explore new behaviors in conflict situations, finish this line as a creative rehearsal of new ways of responding to others:

"When I am angry, I want to try . . ."

55

1. Ernest Bruder, *Ministering to Deeply Troubled People* Englewood Cliffs, N.J.: Prentice Hall, 1963), pp. 30-31.
2. Frank Kimper, "Love and Anger," unpublished manuscript, School of Theology at Claremont, California, 1971. Used by permission.
3. Harry Stack Sullivan, *The Psychiatric Interview* (New York: W. W. Norton, 1954), pp. 218-219.
4. *Ibid.,* p. 109.

Getting Unstuck:
Experiencing
the Freedom to Change

i should
change... (but i
can't.)

i ought
to be
better... (but i'm
helpless.)

i wish
things were
different...(but it's
hopeless.)

what do
i really
want?... (to play
helpless
hopeless
and say
"i can't.")

It's 2 A.M. You're stark awake, lying in bed reliving the day's work. You give up trying to sleep, stick a leg out of bed . . . walk out to the living room . . . oooh . . . you kick a toe against a piece of furniture in the dark.

Then you stand, rubbing your foot, looking out at the lights of the city. So this is what you get. You drive yourself all day. Can't sleep nights. Is this all life has for you? Long days? And even longer nights? Where's the enjoyment, the sense of meaning you once felt? "God, there's got to be more to life than this senseless routine."

You stop suddenly, surprised to discover that you're praying. "I feel so . . . God but I feel alone. If I could just talk this out with my wife, if I had just one friend who mirrored what I feel. . . . I need something, someone to talk with. . . . Where do I start?"

That is when you know. You start where you are. Alone. Hurting, but facing yourself. Reaching out to God.

* * *

Focus your mind on one of your friends. Choose a friend whom you respect most. Someone who has gifts you admire, convictions you envy, and the courage to live them now.

There. You have a face in mind.

Now let's imagine what that person might make of your life if he had the opportunity.

Are you ready for the fantasy?

It's morning. You've just pasted your toothbrush and begun a vigorous brushing when you catch sight of yourself in the mirror. It is not your familiar face that peers back, but your friend's. The toothbrush clatters into the basin. You stand, openmouthed in dazed unbelief. How often you've said, "I wish I were in his shoes for just one day, and he in mine. I'd like to see him face what I put up with every day."

Now it's happened. Somewhere, just now, he's facing your face in the mirror, going down to eat your breakfast, driving your car to your job. He's interacting with your friends, living today with the results of your decisions made in a thousand yesterdays.

The best man you know has just moved into your life, where it is, as it is.

What changes will he make?

Will his fresh viewpoint make a real difference?

Will a new spirit of hope and optimism infect your job, your friends, your work?

Will the abandonment of worn-out habits of thought and action make a change in your life, and the lives of your associates?

Will one day's practice of new behavior patterns

really make a difference in the world you normally touch?

What are the differences? Are they differences you want now? Changes you need now?

What is stopping you from making those changes? How are you keeping yourself from being the different person your work needs, your world needs, you need?

How are you stopping yourself?

You are stopping yourself from becoming all you can be.

You are free to change, if you choose. Change as a person, change in your power-to-live, change in claiming your potentials.

Not to become someone else—as in the fantasy. But to become you. The "you" you really are and can be.

* * *

A police car pulls up under the street light in front of the town hall-police station combination in a small Midwestern town. Two deputies pull a disheveled girl from the back seat. She flinches under their rough handling.

A crowd of men follow them into the office of the Justice of the Peace.

"We caught this hippie slut sleeping in a haystack with two long-haired apes. They got away. But she's gonna get it for all three of 'em."

"Whatta we do to her?" someone asks.

"Wait'll the J.P. gets here; we'll find out."

"The little tramp. She oughta be horsewhipped to

an inch of her life. That usta be the law around here."

A man pushes through the crowd. He kneels beside the terrified, weeping girl.

"Have a little pity," he says gently, looking up at the hard, leering circle of faces.

"Okay, stranger," a deputy demands. "What do you say we do to her? We caught her in the hay with a couple of horny hippies. Don't you think she oughta have it beaten out of her?"

The man straightens up. "The one of you who is without fault, let him strike the first blow," he says evenly, looking from face to face.

An old man is first to leave. Then another. And others. The room empties. Only the man remains with the girl, still lying sobbing on the floor.

"Where are all your accusers?" the man asks. "Has no one struck you?"

"No, no one," she replies.

"I don't condemn you either," he says gently. "You may go. You're not stuck to the old script. You're free to live, a new way. You don't need to repeat all this again." (Compare John 8:1-11.)

* * *

Can people change? Can life be new? Can life be different?

Wrong questions. Wrong words. Wrong viewpoint. It's not "can we" but "will we."

Strength is available. Change is possible. Whenever a man or a woman accepts responsibility for where he is (that's often called confession) and chooses to

63

make a change (that's often called repentance) and reaches out for the strength of God and the accepting love of some significant other persons (that's often called conversion), then change begins.

Yesterday I hurt a friend with quick words that cut too deeply. I am responsible for that. I am choosing to relate to that person in a more gentle way in the future. I am responsible for this new way of behavior.

This is repentance.

I own responsibility for my part in what was unsatisfactory behavior. I accept responsibility for my part in what was unsatisfactory behavior. I accept responsibility for my part in what is and what will be new behavior.

Repentance is owning responsibility for what was, accepting responsibility for what is, and acting responsibly now.

Repentance is responsible action. It is not a matter of punishing ourselves for past mistakes, hating ourselves for past failures, and depressing ourselves with feelings of worthlessness.

Repentance is becoming aware of where my responsibility begins and ends, and acting responsibly.

Repentance is finishing the unfinished business of my past and choosing to live in new ways that will not repeat old unsatisfactory situations.

* * *

I know a mother who recently discovered that her daughter, the second of twins, had lived fourteen years under the burden of a casual comment. "We

64

weren't expecting twins, so the second one came as a great shock," the daughter had heard the mother confide. It was her earliest memory. Feeling unwanted, she withdrew. The mother, not understanding, left her to her loneliness.

Now that she's aware, what's the mother to do? Punish herself for her lack of awareness? Hate herself for the damage done to a sensitive girl?

Neither of these are helpful to either.

She can repent. Which is to own the responsibility for her part in neglecting and ignoring her daughter. And be responsible now. She can say, "I wanted you. You are precious. I want to be close to you now." And act responsibly now. She can plan new ways of being close, new times for listening and conversation, new ways of reaching out to say, "I care. Watch me. See how much I care."

* * *

I know a father who has sat helpless while his sons were growing through their teen-age years. "They won't obey me. There's nothing I can do. I'm a failure as a dad," he would say.

Meanwhile, the boys grew bitter at his lack of strength, his unwillingness to stand up to them, his softness when challenged.

What's the father to do?

He can repent. Which is to own his responsibility for copping out on his sons, recognize how he is avoiding all confrontation with them, and stand up alongside them.

He can care enough to confront them with his own

strength. (He has strength enough. He's been using a lot of it to protect himself.) He can love them enough to let them test their budding strength against his, prove their decision-making ability by matching it with his.

This is repentance. Owning responsibility for what has been, wasting no time in self-punishment or self-hate, and getting on with the kind of behavioral changes that accept responsibility for what really is now, and what can be.

For example, you can say, "I'm sorry, I was wrong. I made a mistake. I'm starting over." Or if your life-style has been a constant apology for living, you're free—in grace—not to apologize, to say, "I'm accepted. I'm all right now. It's okay to be me. I don't need to apologize for living. I'm loved."

The capacity to repent determines our capability to love and forgive, and our ability to receive love and accept forgiveness. It is the growing person who can honestly say, "I have done wrong. I own it. It was my action. I am responsible for it. I am choosing to end that way of behaving. I am choosing to live in a new way."

The capacity to repent is directly related to our willingness to see. You've got to see how it really is before you can truly take repentant responsibility. It takes courage to see what truly is in our relationships. We are afraid and rightly so. Usually we are afraid for the wrong reason.

We tell ourselves, "If I let myself see what really is, all will collapse." It is not so. We can dare to see things as they are, as far as we can be aware, and see we must. It's the only way to grow.

66

Our real fear could well be that things will not collapse, that things will not change, that we're likely to repeat the same errors over and over again, that unless we own our mistakes responsibly, and take responsibility to change, we'll be stuck forever where we are now.

* * *

"Somewhere along the way, I missed it," you say. You're standing in the doorway to your son's room, looking at the empty bed. It's 2 A.M. God knows where he is. Or what he's up to now. "I don't know how or where it started, but I blew it as a dad. I really blew it."

You stand, head against the doorframe, going back through the past seventeen years, wishing you'd done the other thing. Any other thing. And hurting. Hurting for your son and for yourself.

So here you are stewing in your own guilt over mistakes you made in parenting. When wrong and guilt and anger build to the breaking point, you take it out on your son again.

"What if I told him where I hurt instead of telling him what's wrong with him?" you ask yourself. "What if I told him that I care instead of cutting him down? But I have all these mixed-up feelings inside. I need someone to talk with. I need to get my own guts straight again. . . ."

Break the old cycle of—I feel guilty about my son—so I get angry at my son—so I feel guiltier and I get angrier. Admitting where you are—honesty—is the first step to freedom. Accepting responsibility for your past actions is the second.

Then tell your son how you plan to change. Let him know you care. That's what the Bible calls repenting. Asking God's forgiveness for what is past. Drawing on God's strength to change now.

* * *

Repentance—in the full Christian meaning of the word—is a process. It's a thawing out of rigid lifestyles into a flowing, moving, growing, repenting process.

Repentance is living in the open honesty called vulnerability. Repentance is growing in the decisive honesty we call responsibility. Both of these are processes. They continue as long as life continues.

To be a repenting person, I choose to live in open, honest vulnerability before both God and man, and in clear, decisive responsibility to both God and man. This is repenting as a growing life-style. It is growth.

Vulnerability is letting repentance touch my defenses. Responsibility is letting repentance temper my decisions.

A word on vulnerability.

If I need to admit to you that I make mistakes, I freeze up. Until I repent.

If I am about to be honest about my failures, my sudden fear is that I will lose your respect, your trust, perhaps your friendship. It's not true, of course, but my inner defenses keep telling me that it is so.

But repenting—honest owning of my own vulnerability—instead creates trust, makes respect possible, and builds friendship.

(I speak not of self-depreciation done either in self-hate or false humility, but of simple owning of my own experience for what it is.)

Repentant vulnerability is, I discover, the most consistently beautiful and meaningful experience in human relationships. People are lovable when vulnerable. People are believable when vulnerable.

People come to life as real, living, breathing, hurting, feeling, laughing, singing, growing beings when they are vulnerable.

But the price is practicing a life-style of repenting, not pretending. No person ever achieves safe-and-serene invulnerability. But we can pretend it. We can dream that it is possible, work to make it probable in our own lives, and carry on as if we are carrying it off.

But we never arrive. Our pronouncements continue to be questioned. Our pretenses are constantly suspect. Our claimed expertise is never beyond criticism.

We are vulnerable. We feel it even as we deny it.

We might as well affirm it. Own our vulnerability.

Vulnerability is letting repentance replace my old defense strategies with simple honesty, simple openness, simple willingness to change and grow.

Second, a word on responsibility.

Responsibility is letting repentance touch my decisions and turn my actions in new directions.

Repentance is responsible action. As I say this, I am aware that most persons hear the word "responsible" as a command, "You're responsible," made by some authority—either conscience within us or some controlling force without.

But the real meaning of the word is response-ability —the ability to respond. Persons with responsibility are persons in touch with their own ability to respond to others in free, vulnerable honesty.

I am finding that as I choose to be vulnerable to others in admitting who I am, where I've failed, how I hurt, and what I truly want in life, that the strength to respond in new ways—the response-ability—is there. Some of it is my own strength. Much more of it is the strength of God's Spirit within. (Who of us knows where the one ends and the other begins. We are only thankful that strength, courage, endurance, and patience are there. These are the abilities-to-respond.)

Repentance—open vulnerability, honest response-ability—is a continuous, ongoing process in Christian living. I want it to be at the center of my lifestyle. It's the key to growth, to relationship, to witness to God's work in human experience.

Repentance is hope. Hope that change is possible. Hope that I can be forgiven, loved, accepted by both God and my fellows if I only own what I've done and where I am. Hope that life can be new.

The capacity to see clearly where you are . . .

The responsibility to own fully what you've done . . .

The willingness to act decisively now in new ways . . .

The courage to follow through in new behavior . . .

This is repentance. Active (not passive). Acting

(not just thinking, or feeling). Acts! (Not just good intentions or fine emotions.)

I've repenting to do, daily. I expect you may have a bit of it to do too.

I'm expecting it of myself. It's the natural order of things for the growing person. Owning what and where I've been, choosing what and where I shall be going.

Expect it of yourself. Plan it for yourself. Make it a normal part of living. Risk it. It's the key to life.

When Jesus came among us men, His first words were, "The kingdom of God is at hand" (the kingdom of right relationships is here). "Repent and believe the gospel" (turn, change, believe that you are free to love and be loved).

As Phillips translates these words, " 'The time has come at last—the kingdom of God has arrived. You must change your hearts and minds and believe the good news' " (Mark 1:15, *Phillips*)

* * *

The wino looked up as he felt the hand on his shoulder. A dozen men had walked into his alley, stopped, circled around him.

"Sir," one said to the man who seemed to be in charge, "Whose fault is it that this man is a wino? His own? Did his wife drive him to drink? Or was it his parents?"

"Forget the blaming games," the leader replied. "Ask instead, Where can he go? What can he do now?"

Reaching out, he touched his fingers under the man's stubbly chin. Their eyes met, caught, held.

"Come on," he said, "you're free to leave skid row. Here's a five. Go on over to the 'Y,' shed your rags, shower, shave, and go home."

Two hours later, the man got off the bus in his old neighborhood.

"Hey, look. Isn't that Wino Willie?" an old neighbor asked.

"Can't be," another replied. "He's rotting in some alley by now."

"Sure looks like him."

"Yep," says Willie, "it's me!"

"What happened?"

"Dunno. This man says to me, 'Willie, you're free. Go on home. You're okay again!' I did. Here I am. I'm okay."

By this time a crowd has gathered. Family, old friends, two social workers, a probation officer, several local clergymen, a news reporter.

"What's going on?" they all ask. "What's with you?"

"Well, nine o'clock this morning I'm just sleeping off my hangover from last night's half gallon of muscatel, and I'm feeling like the DT's are coming back, when this guy and his friends come up the alley. He talked to me like I was people. Told me I'm okay. Said I was free to put the old life behind me. I could go. I did. Here I am."

"You're putting us on," someone yelled.

"Yeah, it's a hoax. You were no wino. What's your angle?"

"No angle," the guy replies. "I've been splotched for years. Now I'm sober."

"Impossible," a clergyman snapped. "Once an alcoholic, always an alcoholic."

"Could be," the man replies. "This I do know. Once I was wet, now I'm dry."

"Tell us again what happened," the crowd demanded.

"Why? Are you open to changing too? You want to taste a little of this freedom to be different?"

"Change? Nothing doing! You can't change human nature. You're no different. Just wait and see. You're Wino Willie and you always will be! Get out. Go back where you came from."

The downtown bus pulls in. Willie shrugs his shoulders, gets on.

Back on the city street, one block from the bus depot, Willie runs into the man and his group of friends.

"They say I'm no different, that I can't change," Willie says. "I guess they're right. There really isn't any hope."

"What do you think?" the man asks.

"Me? I dunno. But I felt today like I really am different, like God touched me, like I really can be free. Like it's okay to be me."

"That's all true. You can go on being free. And God is with you, see?"

"Yes, I think I see. But my family, my friends, why don't they see it?"

"None are so blind as those who will not see!" (Compare John 9:1-41.)

For Further Thought

1. When you feel you're up against a wall, and unable to change, consider Saint Francis of Assisi's classic prayer:

God grant me the serenity
To accept the things I cannot change,
The courage to change the things I can,
And the wisdom to know the difference.

Exercise that wisdom. Which things can you change? How? Here and now? Arrange them in two columns.

I cannot change	*I can change*
my age	my youthfulness
my sex	my awareness of sexuality
my family	my family relationships
_____	_____
_____	_____
_____	_____

2. In owning, repenting, and finishing past experiences affirm to yourself, to a significant other person, to God with this person . . .

(1) I do not deny the facts of my own past experiences, I do not need to overlook them, I will not distort and justify them. They are past expressions of my freedom to be me. They are no-longer-me. I am forgiven. I am free.

(2) I here and now take responsibility for making my own decisions (I want information from others, I want understanding love from those near to me, I want to be aware of the way of Jesus), but I am fully responsible for my choices—satisfying or

not—and I accept the consequences of my own behavior.

(3) I recognize and respond to "God at work within me—giving me both the will to do and the power to perform." I own and choose "to work out this salvation with a proper sense of awe and responsibility" (Philippians 2:12,13, *Phillips*).

5

Giving Trust:
A Two-Way
Venture of Faith

To be trusted,
Trust.

If you wait until
Trust is deserved,
you wait forever.

Trust now.

Someone is waiting
to trust in return.

"Don't trust anyone over thirty," it once was said by those who thought honesty died at twenty-nine.

Then the twenty-year-olds began to discover how hard it was getting through to the twenty-fives.

"Man, you just can't rap with them anymore," they complained. "We just don't read each other at all."

Then the problem appeared further down the age scale. The eighteen-year-olds began to sense how far over the hill these guys were who had passed twenty.

No sooner had the eighteeners pointed this out than they were deflated by the fifteeners. "Just because they can drive, they think they oughta be able to vote. They're too smart for no more than they know."

That's where the twelve-year-olds chipped in. "Those teen-agers are terrible," they said. "Have you ever tried talking to thirteeners? They won't listen to anybody; they say anybody that doesn't listen to them can lump it!"

The ten-year-olds wouldn't stand silent for that. "It's the twelve-year-olds that are a bunch of spoiled brats; they're hardly out of diapers and they want to tell all kids how to do everything. You just can't trust them."

The five-year-olds got in the last word. "It's the first-graders that cause all the problems. Just because they've got an education and can read they think the world is their piece of cake."

(I hear the toddlers have a few complaints to register against the kindergarten kiddies.)

* * *

"I trust you." When I hear—or sense—that message from another person I feel loved, I feel accepted, I feel respected, I feel worthwhile.

"I don't trust you." When I receive that message from someone important to me, I feel disliked, cut off, rejected.

If being trusted is that significant to our own sense of well-being and self-esteem, then a climate of trust is one of the most crucial elements in families and homes.

Trust—breathed in an atmosphere of love—nourishes life like oxygen. Distrust tightens the chest with anxiety, burns in the throat like smog, tears the eyes with its acidity, and poisons the whole person.

* * *

Test it for yourself. Close your eyes. Withdraw into yourself for a moment. Say, "No one trusts me.

No one. I cannot be trusted. By anyone. I am rejected as untrustworthy." What do you feel? There's a
narrowing of the chest, isn't there? A tightness in
breathing. You want to draw in air but it comes hard.
That's anxiety. That's how it feels when we are not
trusted.

A breath of fresh trust can give a person enough
life to go on for days. But deny a child—or a parent
—or any person—of all trust and he starves on the
stale air of suspicion and rejection.

Of course, no one can live without trust. Deprive
another of it and he'll seek it elsewhere, getting it
wherever he can find it. Or he may come to the point
where he says, "I trust no one. No one but me—myself." That too is death.

We need trust, you and I. So do our children. To
refuse to trust is to do violence to our children. It is
coercion. It is starvation. It is saying, "Until you
measure up to my demands, I withhold the breath of
life-nourishing trust from you. When you earn it
again, when I decide you deserve it, I may give it
back."

* * *

"They're a bunch of little devils," your husband
says, as your daughters back their love-bug out of the
drive. "Who knows what they're up to—sleeping
around, popping pills, smoking pot. Either you're
with me—and we crack down on them—or you're
with them. . . ."

You're in a real bind. You love your husband.
You want to stay in touch with him. But you love

your daughters too. Nothing can persuade you to feel so coldly rejecting, so angrily judging as your husband wants you to be.

"I'm not going to reject either side," you tell yourself. Both my husband and my daughters need me. I need them. I won't let his suspicions and anger stop me from giving trust to the girls, nor will I let myself be cut off from him. My daughters' problems are not going to come between us.

How can you give trust to two different sides and yet be trusted by both? By both caring and confronting. By saying, "You really matter to me. I want to be close to you." And at the same time, saying, "I want you to know what I feel, and how I see the differences between us."

* * *

But what if a son—or a daughter—doesn't earn your trust? What if your trust is betrayed?

"I can't trust you anymore," parents often say. That's not true. The word "can't" is false. "I won't trust you anymore" would be a more honest statement.

"Can't" is an irresponsible word. It says, "Circumstances prevent me, others thwart me, you have stopped me. I am not responsible. I can do nothing." When you change the words "I can't" to "I won't" the truth begins to surface bringing responsibility with it.

When does a parent have the right to say, "I won't trust you anymore"? Only when they have come to the end of their parenting. When they choose to say, "Stop the family, I want to get off."

"You don't trust me anymore," children more often say to their parents. That's a line of many meanings.

1. It may say, "I'm confused. I've just betrayed my own ideals. I've done things I'm ashamed of. Tell me that you trust me. I need a breath of trust."

2. Or it may be saying, "I'm angry. You talk about responsibility. But when I want to make a decision you insist on making it for me. I need room to move, to breathe, to be me."

3. Or it can mean, "I'm frustrated. You use your trust to manipulate me. I feel your trust has many strings attached like, 'I'll trust you if . . . and only if . . .' But do you trust my ability to choose what seems right to me?"

4. Or it may mean, "I'm betrayed. You told me you trusted me, so I made the decision that seemed important to me. Now I see you don't respect me or my decision at all. Not at all. You bear-trapped me. You led me to think I was free to choose, then snap. I'm caught and rejected."

5. Or the phrase may communicate, "I'm guilty. I let you down. I admit it. I need my quota of mistakes. If you expect me to be perfect—according to your own standards—then 'trust' is the wrong word for our relationship. 'Obey' maybe, or 'copy.' But is that what you want—a rerun of your life?"

* * *

"You don't trust us anymore," your son says, as

84

you refuse him the car, and demand that he and his brother cancel their plans for a weekend at the beach. He's right. You don't trust him, but you don't want to put it that baldly.

"Trust has got to be earned," you say to yourself. "If the guys want trust, they'll have to prove themselves for the next month." But you know from experience that demanding trust be earned usually ends in mutual distrust and secrecy.

"I could say, 'Fellows, you want us to trust you to use your best judgment. Okay, we will. And we want you to trust us to use our best judgment in setting a few limits. . . .' "

It's possible to affirm trust in your son even while rejecting untrustworthy acts. Saying, "I'm trusting you to try again—in a better way," opens the door to understanding. Trust is love that forgets the past, reaches out here and now to believe and encourage others, and gives them the freedom to grow.

* * *

What does a child mean when he/she says, "You don't trust me"? Perhaps it's simply, "You're cutting me off. Give me a second chance. Stay with me." Whatever the meaning, what can you answer?

You might try something like this:

"Yes, I trust you to use your best judgment. But I know from my own experience that one person's best judgment may not include quite enough important facts of knowledge to be completely dependable. And sometimes it may need buttressing with some help from others—even parents. If it's important to you that we trust you to use your best judgment, will you trust us to use our best judgment in the questions we raise and the suggestions we make?"

That's a long answer to be sure, but it can afford to be, since trust goes both ways. And parents and children must constantly keep it alive and nourish it.

* * *

"So you don't want to be a doctor, or teach. But isn't there some respectable occupation that appeals to you?" You stare at your silent son in total exasperation. "No, man," he says, "I think I'll just drift awhile and look at life, then maybe find a little primitive land somewhere and go back to the soil.

"Keep your dreams of my future. I won't be needing them," your son says. "Working and slaving for forty years in the establishment only earns you ulcers and a taste for tranquilizers. Who needs all that capital to be happy? Who needs all that worry about Dow-Jones' closings? I want to live."

You hear his values. They're worlds apart from your own. Will you respect them? Or try to force him into some position where he has to yield to your values? "Son," you say, "I want to be able to appreciate your values whether I share them or not. And you matter so much to me, I want to know that you can see and respect my values too, even though you disagree with them. . . ."

There are bridges that can reach across any gap, called love. Respect. Empathy. Willingness to see another's point of view.

To build such bridges, begin by canceling some of

your demands and letting the other know you respect his freedom and integrity. Then honestly say where your values are—that's respecting your own freedom and integrity too. Loving and trusting. Caring and honesting. It's the Jesus way of working through differences.

* * *

To be trusted, you must trust. To receive trust from others, you risk trusting them by opening yourself to them. These two go together—trust and openness.

A climate of mutual trust develops out of mutual freedom to express real feelings, positive and negative. As each person moves toward a greater acceptance of his total self, more and more of his/her potential for loving, trusting, responsibility, and growth are released.

And as the trust level rises between parent and child, the willingness to be open with each other increases too. The two go hand in hand. Trust and openness. Acceptance and honesty. Love and risk.

There are risks involved in all love, acceptance, and trust. If I come to understand another's inner world; if I can sense his confusion or his timidity, or his feeling of being treated unfairly; if I can feel it as if it were my own, then a highly sensitive empathy comes into play between us. A rare kind of trusting-understanding develops.

This is far different from the understanding which says: "I know what's wrong with you," or "I can see what makes you act that way."

This trusting-understanding enters the other's world in his or her terms. And that is risky. If I take your world into mine, I run the risk of being changed, of becoming more like you.[1]

* * *

"You quit your job? But that's stupid," you snap at your son.

"You had a good thing going after school and now you drop it. You'll never amount to anything."

"Yeah, well, I just wasn't digging the work anymore. I decided to split," he says.

"That's you!" you say. "You'll never be worth a thing."

"If that's how you say it will be, . . . that's how it will be."

He's shrugging you off coolly, turning away.

You're stuck at the usual impasse.

You writing him off, he tuning you out.

You predicting failure, keeping score on his mistakes, digging at past hurts to prod him along. He fighting back, spiting you at every chance.

Someone's got to break the cycle. Your worst predictions keep coming true, like prophecies that fulfill themselves.

"I've got to take the first step," you say. "The boy doesn't need me on his back. He needs me backing him up with trust and encouragement."

* * *

Trust is a two-way street. Two-way honesty. A refusal to be completely, trustingly honest is to choose distrust, manipulation, coercion, or clever strategies. Trust, by its very nature, aims at interpersonal truth.

Trusting another with the truth about me is the only authentic way of inviting him to share the truth of his experience.

Trusting follows truthing; truthing increases trusting.

We can choose to give trust—if we really want to trust. Trust is love put in action. To love another is to be eager to trust, to extend that trust, to take risks in trusting.

This is not to encourage blind permissive optimism. Trust with integrity is trust with its eyes open. Trust that cares enough to confront the other with his or her responsibility to be honest, frank, totally out in the open. Trust that cares enough to confront the other with his or her responsibility to be honest, frank, totally out in the open with what he or she is choosing to do. But such trust willingly accepts apologies, forgives the past, cancels old debts, and gives the other his or her future back again. That is forgiveness—the willingness to trust another's repentance and to accept that repentance as sincere and genuine.

For example, trust between husband and wife is based on *open love*—clear messages of affection and fidelity, and *open honesty*—clear statements of what I want, how I feel, how I behave and act in all my relationships. Love and honesty are inseparable parts of trust because trust is a relational thing, a two-way experience. It is circular. Continuous. Reciprocal. It is trust—*between*. It is the loving honest exchange of two or more persons as they interact and interrelate.

Trust is not a personal quality, a character trait, a Christian virtue to be possessed and prized. Trust is a relationship of risk and reliability, of honesty with loyalty, of goodness with genuineness. Trust is the basic stuff of family life, of all relationships.

For Further Thought

Trust is an attitude, which though not observable, can be inferred from certain actions we call "trust-behaviors." Check yourself. Which behaviors are characteristic of your relationships?

Distrust	Trust
Constant evaluation of others.	Avoiding all value judgments of persons and personalities.
Judgmental statements directed at persons and personalities.	Objecting to specific behaviors, not the "behavior."
Attempted control of another's actions, words, expression of feelings.	Respect for another's freedom to think, feel, choose.
Use of strategies to get desired outcomes, manipulation or threat.	Simple, honest statements and clear open requests.
Neutrality when feelings get tense.	A willingness to give of yourself when there is risk.
Acting distant and superior when another feels weak or hurt.	Being vulnerable as an equal with equals.
Demanding absolute promises and ironclad guarantees from others.	Allowing room for spontaneous choices, responses and actions.

| Dogmatically asserting your opinions and viewpoints as right and always right. | Giving tentative statements which are open to others' feelings. |

1. Carl R. Rogers and Barry Stevens, *Person to Person: The Problem of Being Human* (New York: Dell Publishing Co., Inc.) pp. 92-94.

6

Ending Blame:
Forget Whose Fault

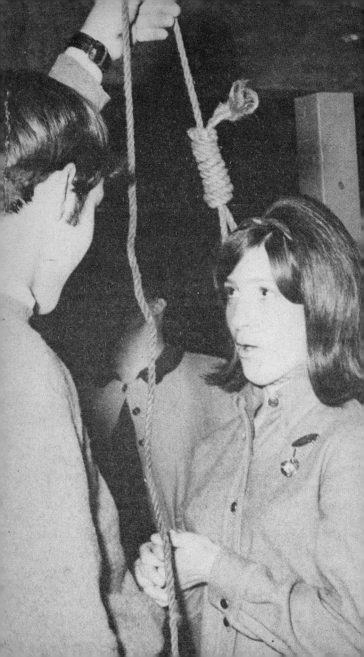

i
blame
you...

...and you
blame
me?

it's
all your
fault...

...it
started
with
me?

it's
your
move
first...

...it's
all
up to
me?

Let's...call
off
the
game.

"Be extra cautious in driving to the market today," a man cautioned his wife one morning. "A friend of mine," he said, "got a ticket yesterday for doing thirty in a twenty miles-per-hour zone."

Later that day, while doing the laundry, she found a receipt for a traffic ticket. The driver had been fined for violating a twenty miles-per-hour speed limit. Without comment, she filed the receipt away in a sugar bowl for future use.

Some weeks later, while pouring her husband's coffee, she said, "Remember that friend of yours who got a ticket on East Market for doing thirty miles per hour? Well, guess what! Yesterday his wife got a ticket for the same reason."

* * *

Nothing ends blaming games like the recognition that the blame must be scored fifty-fifty.

Nothing settles old scores like the recognition that everything finally comes out even. That's how it is, invariably, in a marriage relationship. If there is blame to be fixed, it includes both persons involved.

It takes two people to have a problem. "We" are our problems. The trouble is with "us."

* * *

"I never liked that car—we shouldn't have bought it in the first place," your wife tells you. You're standing in the kitchen holding the crumpled chrome strip you just pulled loose from the smashed fender.

"Why didn't you tell me you scraped the side of the car?" you say low—and with overcontrolled tones.

"It's just the fender. I scratched it."

"Scratched it? Who did you hit? Did you get a ticket? Does he have insurance?"

"Slow down. It was nothing like that. I scraped a post coming out of the parking lot. No accident. No police. No problem."

"Except for our hundred-dollar deductible insurance."

"Hundred-dollar what?"

"Never mind. Where were you looking?"

"Straight ahead. We shouldn't have bought that car to begin with. You paid too much for it. You were taken in. It's never run right. But oh, no. You had to have it. Thought it was sharper looking than Bill's, so you paid through the nose . . ."

"Cut it out!" you bellow. "That's got nothing to do with this fender." You toss the chrome strip onto

97

her white tablecloth. "We're talking about you trying to move a concrete abutment with a Corvette."

"You should be happy I wasn't hurt," she says. "If I were run over by a truck, you'd come into the hospital and throw a greasy fender on my bed."

"Oh, for crying out loud, stick to the problem, will you?"

"That is the problem," she says. "The problem is us. Not a piece of metal."

"The problem is I've got to pay for a smashed fender."

* * *

Both people are involved in the hurt, the problem, the tragedy of a marriage in pain.

Blame is fifty-fifty. In marriage, both people deserve each other. All tends to come out even in the end.

* * *

Example one: "He's the problem," the wife says, "I've given him the best twenty years of my life. I've cared for him in sickness and in health; I've borne him three children; I've never refused him anything. Now look. He betrays me with some little tramp. See how I was wronged?"

Good speech. Good case for scoring the blame ninety-ten. Ninety for him—the villain; ten for her—the virtuous wife. Agreed?

Highly unlikely. When you've heard them both, things even out. Once you see how righteous and superior she appears to him, the score comes nearer fifty-fifty again.

* * *

Example two: "It's all her fault that our son ran away," a husband says. "She nagged at him mercilessly. She criticized his choice of friends. She picked at his hair, his clothes, his way of speaking. She refused to accept the girl he was dating. So the boy left. She drove him away."

He makes a good case for scoring the tragedy ninety-nine to one. Ninety-nine points against her, one for his own responsibility.

But when you've heard both sides, it evens out. In this case, the dad kept his distance from his wife since the boy was quite young. His cool withdrawal taught the boy how to reject, and write his mother off. So the boy did in reality what his dad has been doing all along—withdrawing, rejecting, running away from relationship and intimacy.

* * *

"Trading for this car was your stupid idea," your wife says angrily. "Now we're stuck with the lemon."

"That's not true. We bought the one you wanted."

"We were taken. It's your fault."

You hit the starter one more time. It turns over but with no success.

"You've been had," she says.

You give the ignition key another angry twist. If only it were her ear. She talks you into a car, then blames you for buying it. Or did you buy the one she liked, knowing you could blame her when something goes wrong? Either way, you're both being had in these no-win battles. Somebody's got to make a move for honesty.

"Jill," you say, "we're getting farther apart every time we fight. You're out to win by putting me down. I'm out to win by putting you down. We both lose. I don't care who wins. I just want to be close to you."

There's surprise all over her face.

"That's what I really want, too," she says.

* * *

Whose fault is it when things go wrong? That's the first question we try to answer in many of our difficult moments. For those who prefer placing responsibility elsewhere, the question leads to a wild-goat chase for someone who can be scapegoated with the main load of blame. For those who prefer to sponge up the anger and store it away inside, the blame can be taken heroically upon themselves. "It's all my fault," they say, "I'm the total failure." And even more people do both. At one moment they blame themselves for the whole tragedy, at the next, they take another swing at the scapegoat.

Blaming ourselves is useless, for a variety of reasons.

(1) We usually blame ourselves for all the wrong reasons. (The crucial things that went wrong are not likely to occur to us alone.)

(2) We're not qualified to sit in final judgment of our own lives. We so easily slip into either total re-

jection, "I'm no good at all, I don't deserve to live," or we excuse ourselves lightly, "So what, I'm only human." (To assume the right to sit in judgment over my motives, my past, my true condition is playing God.)

I don't truly understand my past. I know that my memories are selective. I recall those things that fit with my self-image.

Friedrich Nietzsche, the German philosopher, put this pointedly, saying, "Pride and memory had an argument. Memory said, 'It happened thus and so!' Pride replied, 'Oh, but it couldn't have been like that!' And memory gave in."

So it is for us all. Memory gives in, again and again. Most of the pictures we recall from our past have been retouched. Most of the scripts we can quote from old conversations have been edited for us by pride.

Going through our old memories to place blame is like hunting for a black bead in a dark room at midnight wearing heavy gloves and a blindfold.

I want to, rather simply, own my past with as few defenses as possible, and live now in the present before God and with my brothers and sisters.

Recognizing how unable I am to judge myself brings me to awareness of how unqualified I am to judge a sister or a brother. Since my vision is as impaired as though a beam of wood were protruding from my eye, I am poorly equipped to remove splinters from others, as Jesus put it unforgettably.

Pass no judgement,
And you will not be judged.
For as you judge others,

So you will yourselves be judged,
And whatever measure you deal out to others
Will be dealt back to you.
Why do you look at the speck of sawdust
    in your brother's eye,
With never a thought for the great plank
    in your own?
Or how can you say to your brother,
"Let me take the speck out of your eye,"
When all the time there is that plank in your own?
You hypocrite!
First take the plank out of your own eye,
And then you will see clearly
To take the speck out of your brother's.
                  Matthew 7:1-5, *NEB*.

As St. Paul put it:
Love keeps no score of wrongs;
Does not gloat over other men's sins,
But delights in the truth.
There is nothing love cannot face;
There is no limit to its faith, its hope, and its en-
    durance.
             1 Corinthians 13:5-7, *NEB*.

"My knowledge now is only partial," Paul admits. "Someday it will be whole."

It is not perfect knowledge that we need to ask of each other. It is not perfection that we need to demand from those near us, but love.

And love begins by discarding the scorecards. By forgetting whose fault. By forgiving, forgetting the past, and beginning again.

"Love keeps no score of wrongs" (1 Corinthians 13:5, *NEB*).

Love doesn't say, "One for you, one for me, two, three, four for you. Now I've got a couple coming to me."

Love ends the blaming games and gets on to the real questions: What is the loving, responsible, truly respectful thing to do now? Where do we go from here? When do we start? If not from here—where? If not now—when? Who—if not you and me?

This calls for change. Repentance is the name of life without blaming games. It's owning my share of the responsibility to begin again, now. Once more with the help of God.

It's recognizing that whatever the problem between husband and wife, parent and child, it's not one person's fault. It takes two people to have a problem.

It is owning responsibility, breaking the lead from the fine-line bookkeeping pencil, tearing up the scorecard, and beginning again. *Now*.

For Further Experience

1. Discuss a less sensitive difference between you and your wife after covenanting the following ground rules:

(1) All language must be in present tense.

(2) All comments must be here and now.

(3) All statements must begin with "I feel . . ." (And give real feelings, not "I feel *that* . . ." which is a judgment, idea, or criticism masquerading in feeling language.)

103

(4) All blame statements are discarded as soon as either recognizes the finger being pointed.

Now move on up to a slightly more sensitive beef (or complaint). See if you can maintain clear, simple feeling-wanting statements.

2. Finish the following sentences for each other with at least three endings:
"I appreciate . . ."
"I want . . ."
"I need . . ."
"I demand . . ."
"I resent . . ."

Hear each other. Cancel old hidden demands. Drop blaming strategies and work toward what you truly want for yourself, for each other, for you both together.

7

Case Dismissed:
Reclaiming the Gavel

Order.
Please rise.

The Honorable
Everyman presiding.

You may be seated.

Case one.
Humanity Vs. You.

How do you plead?
Guilty or not guilty?

"What will people think?" you ask your daughter. "What will people say? That kind of thing just isn't done around here. Not by our kind of people. I don't want to hear about it."

You see frustration turning to anger in your daughter's eyes. She's up against the old wall "what will people think?"

You've been banging your head against that wall all your life. In every decision you first consider, "How will it look to others? What will it do to our family name?" How you feel or what you believe matters little when the final choice hangs on others' values.

"Is that what I want for my daughter?" you ask yourself. "Blind obedience to others' expectations? What has it done for me?

"Joanie," you say, "It doesn't matter that much what people will say. Let me hear what you want again. I don't think I was really listening."

* * *

"Wake up," your conscience commands. "It's time to be in court."

"Right, your honor," you reply. Your conscience acts as judge when you're alone. But once downstairs, your wife will occupy the bench. Then, at work, the boss will pick up the gavel. At lunch, Charlie will preside while you tell him about last night's problem with the neighbor who backed over your son's bike. Then, tonight, at home your brother-in-law Pete ("They're coming over for supper, remember?") will be presiding behind the desk.

And you? You're in the docket. On trial. Permanently. One judge follows another. The evidence is heard. You testify—often against yourself. The sentence is passed—"guilty," or "not guilty." And your case is passed on to the next judge.

You know the feeling?

The feeling of being constantly on trial?

The feeling that life is not a stage—but a courtroom. That others have been appointed to judge. And you? You're the judged. Always on trial.

And you put yourself there on the stand, in the stocks, or at the gallows with the noose around your neck.

You are handing out gavels.

You can quit.

* * *

"Claiming love for yourself is the real secret," Dr. Frank Kimper counsels. "There was a time when—

though I was loved, I did not have the courage to claim it. Depressed, lonely, I felt no one cared about me. It wasn't really true, but I lived as though it were; and as a result I was sick at heart and sick in body. I worked for praise, thinking that love had to be earned. I assumed that to be praised was to be loved, and to be criticized was to be rejected. So I was always on trial.'"

* * *

It is painful to be always on trial. You work for praise. Praise is a ruling in your favor. Enough praise might add up to an acquittal. And a little more than enough praise might even convince you that you're okay.

"To be praised is to be loved," you tell yourself. It's not true, of course. To be praised more often is to be manipulated. To be praised is often to be used. To be praised is often to be outsmarted, outmaneuvered, out-sweet-talked. But when you live to be praised, it doesn't matter. No price is too great for a little praise. "Just can't get enough of that praise!"

But when you get it, it's nothing. It turns to ashes in your teeth. You work for praise and approval, live for approval and praise, even sacrifice just for praise and approval. And what do you have to show for it? Emptiness. Loneliness. And little of the love you wanted so much.

Because the other side is there to haunt you. Criticism. And to be criticized is to be rejected. To be criticized is to lose approval, respect, love, and everything you're working toward.

110

That's not true either, of course. To be criticized is often to be truly appreciated. To be respected so much that the other person can share both his positive and his negative feelings about you. To be criticized by a real friend is to be loved.

But when you put yourself on trial, criticism is rejection and praise is acceptance.

What a way to live! What a way to not live. To be constantly on trial is not living. It is existing as a shadow, a reflection of others' approval or disapproval.

It can all end whenever you want it to. No one is constantly on trial unless she or he chooses to be. If you live for another's praise, or cringe rejected under another's criticism, you are choosing to be on trial. You volunteer to be victim.

To measure your own worth or to feel yourself a person of worth only when the respect is coming in, is giving others far too much power.

You are you. Claim yourself. Be who you are. You are a person of worth. Own yourself. Recognize what you are. Reclaim the power to be who you are in spite of your moment-to-moment performance, regardless of your day-to-day achievements. Be who you are before God and man.

* * *

Think of those persons whose approval is all-important to you. Do you see their approving or judging faces? Now—in your mind—go to each one of them. Say, "I have given you the power to reject me. When you reject me, I reject myself. When you approve of me, I approve of myself. My happiness, well-being, and self-respect depend on your approval."

It sounds so stupid to actually say those things aloud, doesn't it? But go ahead. Finish it. Say to that face who is now frowning at you, "I reclaim my responsibility for me. I am no longer giving you the power to reject me, and cut me off from love, joy, and happiness. I am re-owning myself."

Now you're facing the real issue. Will you accept love from others without needing first to pay for it in advance? Without needing first to earn it—then receive it? Will you claim love for yourself? Will you bear to be loved—whether you feel you deserve it or not?

We're at a very crucial point here. Accepting love. For many it's unpalatable. Unacceptable. Love is only to be accepted in return for work well done. I've been there myself. Even when I was told I was loved whether my performance matched all expectations or not, I didn't believe it. I explained it away. When others affirmed me as someone who is loved, I rationalized it off. It only made matters worse to be loved.

Until I claimed it. Accepted it. Received it gratefully. No questions asked.

That's the real meaning of what the New Testament calls "grace." To be loved—and to need to accept that love—right at the point where we don't deserve it.

But God, rich in mercy, for the great love He bore us, and the immense resources of His grace, and great kindness to us in Christ Jesus, made us His own. By His affection unearned you are forgiven. It is not your own doing. It is God's gift, not a reward for work done. There is nothing for anyone to boast of. (See Ephesians 2:4-10.)

Do you respond to love like that? Do you say, I am prized? I am a precious person? I am valued, loved, accepted, forgiven? Then you are no longer on trial before God.

Will you step into the same kind of relationship with others? Accept the freedom of loving and being loved without feeling always in the docket, always self-conscious, always on trial.

* * *

"You mean I'm not on trial?"
"Only if you put yourself on the block."
"And I needn't fear you as my judge."

"I don't want the job. Reclaim your power to be you. Affirm your freedom to be yourself. Your trial is over."

* * *

You're driving alone. The hours stretch long. You find yourself talking out loud—to you. But you're not sure you know the other half of you that answers back. At times you feel so rejected, so cut off, so lonely, so isolated from others. You don't feel understood. You hardly understand yourself. . . .

It's a strange feeling, recognizing that you've been out of touch with your own deep need to feel really understood, and accepted, and at peace with yourself, to feel right with the universe.

While you're talking out loud, try saying some of those things to God. Put out your deepest feelings. Then say what you really want. Describe the kind of love and acceptance you'd want from Him if He were here.

When it's all out on the dashboard, then experience the silence. The openness. The release. Then listen. Feel. Reach out. You may now be in touch with what you've really been wanting all along. Wanting to know that you are loved. To be sure that you are accepted.

* * *

I like you as you are
Exactly and precisely
I think you turned out nicely.[2]

This song lyric by the Reverend Fred Rogers is a favorite of the little people who watch his award-winning children's TV program, *Mister Rogers' Neighborhood.*[2] They're favorites of children from three to ninety-three.

What more do you want of life than love, acceptance, respect for what you are, and personal appreciation?

If such love comes only as we earn and deserve it, I have a feeling I'm not the only one who must be counted out. Even perfect people have their problems in measuring up. No one knows his own failings better than the perfectionist himself. I know that firsthand. I used to be one myself.

Perhaps you have moments when you become aware of how little you deserve the love, acceptance, respect, and personal appreciation you want—and need.

To know that you're rejectable, and sometimes to agree that you deserve rejection, hurts. And hurts where nothing much helps. It hurts because deep inside you fear that if the truth were known, if justice were done, if all scores were settled, you'd be lost.

That's the feeling. A feeling of great loss. Of loss of all that is most valuable, of yourself. "I" am lost. "I am rejected of God," you may feel. Right at this point, the best word you could hear would be,

You are accepted—as you are.

You are loved—for what you are.

You are respected—in spite of what you are not.

God appreciates you, if you can receive it. He can and does say, "I love you, I accept you, you are loved." And He speaks such love, knowing exactly what—or whom—He is accepting. He understands the full cost of such an act. So when He says, "I like you as you are, exactly and precisely," He does it open-eyed. His love is not blind.

And yet, His love voluntarily blinds itself to the failures of our past. When He forgives, and we accept that forgiveness by letting it become real in our own forgiving attitudes toward ourselves and our fellows, then the old situations become forgettable. He ignores them. They are forgotten.

To accept acceptance, when we know that we are unacceptable, is for many an unbearable, impossible task.

To receive help and to need to admit that we cannot help ourselves is no easy thing. For many it's an unpalatable thing that they simply will not endure. So they must stay stuck with their feelings of rejection, hung up with the need to pay their own way, frozen at the one point of great opportunity. And there they stay. Stuck. Painful feeling. I once hung there myself.

No words effectively describe the sense of freedom that comes when you finally let go.

No language expresses the experience of being accepted, of knowing that you are accepted, of accepting that acceptance.

To accept another's acceptance at the moment you see yourself as unacceptable, this is grace. And grace received is experienced as joy.

To give joy to another is to extend grace—love without conditions and limitations—to another. It is to admire, appreciate, and enjoy another without trying to change him or her by rejecting parts of that person as unacceptable or intolerable.

To enjoy another is like enjoying a sunset. You do not command, "Tone down the reds. Raise the lavenders. Stop! Too much yellow. A bit more blue, please." You are not in command. You are in awe. In respect. In appreciation. And to see another person unfold and to enjoy that unfolding—that is grace.

Joy happens when we can truly accept another— and are accepted. Have you not experienced joy when you come close enough to another that he can see into your soul. "What if I am unacceptable? What if I am rejected?" we wonder in fear. And, at the moment when you expect rejection, you discover the joy of appreciative acceptance in the other's smile.

Joy happens when we can truly love another—warts, faults, quirks and all. Have you not experienced it when a friend comes close enough to see faults and blemishes, as well as virtues and strengths, and still loves you? "He knows what I'm really like. She knows me for what I truly am. Yet I am loved," you say. That's grace.

Joy happens when we can truly hear another, and be truly heard. Have you not experienced joy when a friend shows you that he cares in the only believable way—by hearing not just your words, but hearing you. And your heart wants to shout, "I've been heard. Someone else knows what it's like to be me." You feel it in the chest and around the eyes. It's a moistness. Like tears. Tears of joy.

Joy is the enjoyment of being enjoyed.

Grace is the acceptance of being accepted. To experience acceptance is to experience grace.

Love is seeing another as precious, just as you know yourself to be precious.

For Further Thought

1. Do you tend to feel judged and condemned when you hear how others see you, what they expect of you, and where they differ or disapprove? Go to that person in your imagination and say, "I hear your expectations. I am not responsible for them. I want to be who I am and still be in relationship with you. I am responsible for that."

2. Will you affirm—When I have chosen to act according to my values . . .

(1) I will not reject or regret my action mere
because someone has passed judgment or volu
teered criticism against it.

(2) I will not disown, deny, or feel a need
make excuses or justify my behavior.

(3) I will change my ways of behaving out of
spect for others' feelings and rights, or because
am finding more satisfying ways of relating to ot
ers—but not out of fear of their judgment or ce
sure.

3. Say these affirmations to someone you love:

(1) I am equally precious, as you are preciou
Our abilities may differ; our worth, never.

(2) I no longer question my worth as a pers
even when I feel others may.

(3) When you criticize me, I will see you as c
ing and confronting me. I want to hear the cri
cism, and not feel attacked or rejected. When y
praise me, I will say a simple, "Thank you."

---

1. Frank W. Kimper, *Meditations for Churchmen in the 7*
2nd ed., STC, Claremont, California 1971.
2. *I Like You As You Are* (Josie Carey—Fred Roger
Copyright ©1959 Vernon Music Corporation. Internatio
copyright secured. All rights reserved. Used by permission
the copyright owner.

8

Prejudice:
What Has It Done
for You Lately?

I'M NOT PREJUDICED...
(but keep them
off my block.)

I'M NO BIGOT...
(but let them have
their own church.)

I'M AS TOLERANT
AS THE NEXT...
(but would you want
your daughter to marry one?)

"Talk about going after every cent you got," you say to the guys over lunch. "You gotta count you fingers to see if you've got 'em all when you leav that Jewish clothing store at the mall."

You grin appreciatively as the fellows chuckl Then it hits you. That line was a direct quote fror long ago by your dad. A rerun of his racial feelings.

"I don't dig my replaying my dad's racist lines, you admit to yourself, "but it's a matter of habi Those old family scripts get rerun in me like the were on tape. And I don't recognize the stale dia logue until I hear it out loud.

"I'm going to start listening for those old tapes, you decide. "When I hear them, I can stop, even it's in the middle of a line, and start over. I'm nc stuck with the prejudiced attitudes I caught at hom I can choose my words. I can choose new ways c feeling toward people of different racial back grounds. . . ."

* * *

Where did you first get the idea
That blacks are different,
That Indians don't matter,
That Japanese make cheap junk,
That Mexicans are lazy,
That Polacks are stupid,
That Russians are malicious,
That Italians are emotional?

Where did the ideas begin? I can't recall who first implanted the stereotypes in my mind. Can you identify how they first came to you?

How you got your prejudices is not the crucial thing now. Why you still have them is what hurts.

If the stereotypes of prejudice are with me now, I am responsible. If they are still with you, you are responsible. Such ideas stay with us because we choose to keep them with us. We reindoctrinate ourselves with strange ideas such as these:

"Black people are biologically different from whites."

"Minority people are shiftless, lazy, and not to be trusted."

To keep alive such flimsy excuses as though they were facts, we have to keep repeating them, keep telling ourselves that they are true, keep saying them in daily conversations:

"Minority children have low IQ's."

"The Indian has contributed little to our world."

"The race problem in America is a black problem."

123

"The race problem in Canada is an Indian problem."

The words are empty. We know it, so we say them twice as often to convince ourselves that our prejudices are still serviceable.

They aren't.

* * *

You met the Roberts at a neighbor's backyard barbecue. They were the first blacks you ever knew —on a personal, family, social basis. You enjoyed them. But you were uncomfortable. You caught yourself checking on how the man was looking at your wife. You felt yourself anxious and distant.

So you're just becoming aware of how deep your prejudice runs? You do buy into the old stereotypes—like blacks are sexual athletes, they aren't safe around white women, they have no motivation to work, their fingers are long. "Where do all these old lines come from?" you wonder.

"From me," you admit. "They're part of my memory bank. I call them up. I reindoctrinate myself, reaffirm such ideas each time I think or mouth them. Maybe if I talked about my prejudices with the Roberts themselves, they could help me.

"Me? Receive help from a black?" There's another old line again. "Yes. Why not?" you say.

* * *

What I carry with me into the next moment is my choice. What prejudices and ideas I keep with me as baggage are my responsibility. But I am free—if I'm willing to accept the freedom God gives—to leave the past and its opinionated, bigoted, self-serving opinions and ideas behind me. Unless I insist on holding them close.

I have racist attitudes. I don't like them when I discover them in myself. I've hidden and denied them. Now I know that healing comes as I can own these attitudes, admit my inner confusion, confess my apathy, discard my myths, and make a change.

Life changes from moment to moment. I too can change. Unless I choose to be stuck, to stick by old, narrow, self-defeating ideas and ways of behaving. Healing can come as I become willing to risk the pain of letting go of what I've clung to.

Or hung onto. Prejudice is a bulldog grip. It is clenched teeth. It is a spiteful bite that grips the past and its stale ideas as a protection against the present and its realities. It is hanging onto the imaginary security of fantasies that "me and my kind" are superior.

Healing follows a willingness to risk exposing how wrong I've been. We can let healing, forgiveness, love, and reconciliation happen. It's up to us to allow them to course through our lives, as a gift of God's grace. Or to refuse them, as we more often do.

* * *

"Hey," your neighbor asks, "the black guy on your work crew? What's his name?" You stand there, dumbfounded. Sure, you know all three guys' names, but for the moment, you can't recall which one is black. You grin, surprised at yourself. You'd avoided the guy at first. Now, Greg—that's his name—is the man you feel closest to of the whole crew.

"When you learn to know and appreciate a man complexion doesn't matter much," you tell you neighbor. "For the moment, I couldn't remember which of the three is black. It's Greg, of course. He's the best of the three."

"That's the trouble with getting too close to them," your neighbor responds. "You get to thinking you're all the same, and you're not."

"Yes, we are," you say. "When Greg and I began working together, I was actually afraid of him, and tried to keep a kind of superior distance. But now, admire the guy. I've learned a lot from him. He's inferior to no one, you and me included."

* * *

What is prejudice doing for you? What has it done for you lately?

What are we doing with our prejudices that we defend them so well and maintain them so efficiently Let's be specific. When I say "Chicano," what image do you have? Of a short, fat, chili-and-tortilla-eating, lazy, uneducated Mexican-American?

That is false. Chicanos do not breakfast on hot tamales. Chicanos are as concerned with life-work education-community relationships as any other group of comparable social and economic level Chicanos have as much to contribute as any other ethnic group in America. We will all be made poorer if we refuse to receive it.

When I say "Indian," what image do you have? Of a shifty, dishonest, alcoholic, sponging savage who lives on government money? That's untrue, unfair, unfeeling, and unfounded. Indians have made as great a contribution to our cultures as any group in Canada or the United States.

What are we doing with such prejudices? May I suggest we are excusing ourselves for (1) being unmoved by injustice done to others, (2) withdrawing from human need into indifferent safety, (3) enjoying our wealth without admitting that our gain often demands another's loss, (4) demanding government programs that profit our kind and class while depressing others. And that's only the beginning.

What are your prejudices doing? What have they done for you lately?

Excused indifference about the whites-only policy in your neighborhood, apartment building, business, or club?

Justified your doing business with restaurants, barber shops, motels, and recreational facilities that welcome only white-Anglo-Saxon-worthies?

Maintained your church as a lily-white organization supporting the status quo?

Bolstered sagging self-confidence, by putting down those who are never present to defend themselves?

What function do prejudices perform for you? They serve some end, or they would likely be dropped and forgotten. Become aware of what you're doing with your collection of racial labels and stereotypes. When you become aware—truly aware —of what you are doing and how you are doing it, you have a choice. You can choose to quit it. Or you can choose to excuse it and continue it. But at least you have the choice.

* * *

"Just because you're white and I'm black, is no reason for me to hate you," Jim, your fellow workman, says. "We're brothers, as far as I'm concerned. How you feel is up to you."

You see the acceptance in his eyes. Suddenly you're jealous of his freedom to accept himself, as he is—and others, like you, as you are.

"Now that I've dealt with my hate problem," Jim was saying, "I can be black and beautiful, and you can be white and powerful, and it's all the same to me."

What he's saying sounds good—and feels good to you, but you're still stuck in old, stale feelings that whites are whites and blacks are blacks, and acceptance and mutual appreciation just don't figure in. "If I could be free to accept others, like you do," you say, surprised at your own honesty. "But where do I begin?"

"You're doing great," he says. "Just keep on asking questions like that. Keep on listening. Keep on trying to understand others. And it'll come to you. . . ."

* * *

Let your mind float freely for the next minute, and fantasize with me . . .

It's morning. You're rubbing the sleep from your

eyes, after punching the alarm clock to silence, when you notice your hands. They're brown. Not their natural tan but a deep dark brown. (Or if you're naturally black, imagine that the hands you hold in front of your eyes are suddenly white.)

You stumble out of bed and stand staring in dumb disbelief into the mirror. You're black. (White.) Overnight through some unexplainable freak act of fate you've become another, the other race.

The bacon-coffee smells of breakfast tell you that your wife is in the kitchen. What will she say or do as you enter? Will her eyes scream rejection? Will she recover with that phony smile (too wide, too long, too many teeth showing) that speaks rejection while it signals acceptance? The smile you've often given to people of other races?

The men in your car pool, they'll be stopping by for you in thirty minutes. What will they say? And at the office, will there be a new distance separating you from your fellow workers? Will the job still be yours by tonight?

What of your friends? Will they be just as close as before? Your racist brother-in-law, how will you get along with him? And then there's your church, will you be welcome now? Or will the cold shoulder move you on to the side aisles and out of the door in a short time?

You look closely at yourself in the mirror. You've got to go out and face the world, but right now you're not happy about facing yourself, about being the self you are now becoming.

* * *

Do you find fantasies such as this distasteful? Threatening? Uncomfortable? Do you prefer to avoid discovery of things about yourself and your feelings toward other races?

To be able to see things from another's point of view is to be truly human, to be fully alive.

To be willing to see life from others' perspectives is to begin to understand them, and to know yourself.

To be concerned about experiencing life from the vantage points—or disadvantage points—of other races and groups is to begin to awaken to life, to the world about you, to responsibility and to love.

To see things from another's viewpoint, to experience his experience, is of value only if you care—if you love enough to be concerned about his welfare as you are about your own.

St. Paul has some incisive words at this point. "Look to each other's interest and not merely to your own. . . . If . . . life in Christ yields anything to stir the heart . . . any warmth of affection or compassion . . . [try] thinking and feeling alike, with the same love for one another, the same turn of mind, and a common care for unity" (Philippians 2:4,1-3, *NEB*).

"None of you should think only of his own affairs, but each should learn to see things from other people's point of view" (Philippians 2:4, *Phillips*).

That's heavy. It says, "Try on your brother's skin. Listen until you hear his point of view. Then get inside it. See how it fits for size. See how it feels to be there where he is. See what love is asking you to do."

Hubert Schwartzentruber, pastor of the Bethesda Mennonite Church in inner-city St. Louis, speaks with a prophetic voice on linking Christian love and understanding to Christian action. The best way to see your brother's needs is to look honestly at your own, and then recognize that the needs of others are identical.

"The best gauge to determine what a man's needs are is to take a look at what one's own needs are. I want to be free to make my decisions. If we then see someone else hindered from making free decisions, we must help to remove that which blocks decision-making and freedom for him.

"If I need a job, then my brother needs one too. . . .

"If I believe that my children need a good education, but many people through no fault of their own do not have my opportunities, then I have an obligation to help make quality education available for their children, too.

"If I have a need for a house for the safety of my family, then I must be concerned about the need of a man who, for a variety of reasons, does not have a safe place in which to house his family. . . .

"If it is for the welfare and the best interest of my family to have health care, then can I be a Christian without also doing something about the needs of those who have no way to obtain proper health care?'"

Asking questions such as these can help us begin to see from the other's point of view.

Seeing life from inside another's needs as well as my own can broaden concern and bring awareness of my responsibility to act.

Feeling life from inside another's skin can shake me loose from complacent enjoyment of my good fortune and calloused indifference to the needs of others.

* * *

You're standing, stunned, hardly believing you've heard your daughter's words.

"Are you saying you love this . . . this . . . ?" You see in her eyes you'd best swallow the racial slur.

"I'm not sure," she replies, "but I think we're in love, perhaps enough to choose to marry."

You, of all people, are suddenly at a loss for words. Of all the men (your kind of men) in this world, your daughter gets involved with this—What do you dare call him?—minority person.

"Would you want your daughter to marry one of them?" you've often asked as a trump question to silence all arguments about races getting close. Now you're facing it yourself. And all the old lines about mongrelizing the races seem useless and empty now that it's your daughter. You could tell her it's beneath her class, that it just isn't done by your kind, that it just won't go in your family. (Not that she'll really listen to all that.)

"No amount of arguments are going to make any difference," you admit to yourself. "Threats will only cut us off. She is her own person. She will need to make her decisions. It is her life."

* * *

Sooner or later, discussions of race boil down to marriage, intermarriage, interracial marriage.

Perhaps you've often used the question to trump any argument. But what do you really feel? What would you actually do if it were you?

Once you put yourself into the real situation, and begin to feel it from within, it's a lot different than the phony, hypothetical "what-if-your-daughter" arguments.

What are the real questions at stake?

Objection one: It's not biblical. Interracial marriage is forbidden by God. All through biblical history, beginning with Cain, God has followed a strict policy of segregation. He called His people the Jews out of other nations, prohibited intermarriage, kept them separate.

Even the most superficial study of the Bible will show that such separation was on religious grounds only. There is not the slightest hint that color, skin, hair, or shape of skull mattered at all. And the list of great men who married across national-racial lines include Abraham, Joseph, Moses, David, and Solomon. (If you are unclear on this, read Numbers 12, and note God's attitudes toward segregationists and critics of intermarriage.)

Did the New Testament oppose racial mixtures? "Yes," say some, quoting St. Paul, "He [God] made of one every nation of men to dwell on all the face of the earth, having determined . . . the bounds of their habitation" (Acts 17:26, *ASV*).

Perhaps you already noticed as I cited this much-quoted passage, that its real point is that "God has made of *one* every nation of men." We have a common Creator, a common ancestry, a common bloodstream, a common destiny.

133

Did Jesus and His disciples teach integration
practice mixing of races?

Consider how Jesus refused to go along with
apartheid policies against Samaria, and how
apostles welcomed Gentiles and Africans, Jews a
Arabs into the new fellowship. There were no fir
and second-class citizens in the new church. (See G
latians 2 and Acts 15.)

There are no biblical arguments against interm
riage. Its message is that all who follow Christ l
come a new race—or better, that we move beyc
all racial and national distinctions and become c
new people—people of God who follow Jesus
Lord. Actually, the Christian faith has no view at
on the problem of race, simply because from
Christian point of view there is no distinction l
tween one man and another that allows one man
be set above another. All men are equal before G
In Christ there is neither Jew nor Greek. For th
who follow Christ, race is a cultural matter of int
est, but of no significance in value, no barrier to
lationships, no block to total acceptance.

Objection two: It's not practical; it can't be s
cessful. It's common sense to oppose interracial m
riage on the grounds that there is too little in co
mon. The customs, values, and interests are differ
—perhaps even the language—so the marriage ca
succeed.

Evidence is to the contrary. Japanese-Americ
marriages, with great cultural and linguistic c
ferences, have a lower divorce rate than all-Ame
can marriages. A study by Thomas Monahan
8,000 interracial marriages in Iowa from 1940

1967, shows that marriages between Negro men and white women are more stable than all-white marriages and twice as stable as all-black marriages. The same findings come from other studies.[2]

Objection three: It's biologically bad. Many whites oppose intermarriage because "racial mixture," they feel, " will lead to the degeneration of the white race."

Dr. Lowell Noble notes on this:

"History reveals that the white man, who seems to regard mongrelization as the worst evil, has in fact, already been responsible for mixing the races. His abuse of the Negro slave woman resulted in thousands of brown or light-skinned Negroes—or should we say dark whites. The logic runs something like this: If the white male is responsible for interracial offspring, no harm is done, since it is the inferior Negro race that is mixed. Such logic is clearly built on white racism."[3]

The biological facts are all to the opposite. Racial mixture neither damages nor improves the offspring.

Objection four: It's wrong for the children. They become outcasts.

Others oppose interracial marriage because the children must suffer greater discrimination. It is not so. All research indicates that the children suffer no more discrimination than any other minority group.

Dr. James Carse, a historian of Christian faith, speaks to this point. "Children of such unions will surely experience considerable hardship and disadvantage, is the most commonly heard argument. The fact is, that the 'hardship and disadvantage' visited upon such children, arise not out of their 'mixed' parentage, but out of their being 'Negro.' Disadvantaged? Indeed, because in his most formative years he has before him the model of two persons who have made an ultimate commitment in the face of an issue that hatred has created, the 'interracial' child is privileged.'"

* * *

Is all this an attempt to give blanket approval to or promote interracial marriage? Not at all. The decision on whom and when to marry belongs to the people entering that marriage.

It is saying several things.

1. Christians—who seriously try to follow Jesus daily in life—will refuse to make distinctions between one race or another, or to make decisions on the basis of one race being imagined as superior to another.

2. Those who follow Jesus point out dishonesty and discard dishonest beliefs as they discover them. And there is no honest base—biblically, biologically, culturally, or statistically, for fighting or prohibiting interracial marriages.

3. Those who follow Jesus will question and challenge prejudices that separate people and walls that create distrust between people.

Look at Jesus Christ.

He was born in the most rigidly ethnic culture of all time; born in a fiercely nationalistic nation; born in Galilee, the most bigoted backwoods of that nation; born into a family of snobbish royal lineage; born in a time when revolutionary fanaticism fired every heart with hatred for the Roman oppressors; born in a country practicing the apartheid of rigid segregation between Jews and Samaritans.

Jesus Christ was born in a world peopled with prejudiced, partisan, fanatical, intolerant, obstinate, opinionated, bigoted, dogmatic zealots—Roman, Samaritan, and Jewish.

Yet He showed not a trace of it.

Read and reread the documents of His life. There is absolutely nothing that you can find to indicate feelings of racial superiority, national prejudice, or personal discrimination.

Those who stand on the side of Jesus Christ reject prejudice whenever, however, and wherever they find it. In themselves first of all; then, and only then, in the world about them.

"No man can know Christ truly except he follow Him daily in life."[5] A life of love. A life of forgiveness. A life of acceptance. As Jesus Christ lived, loved, and died.

For Further Thought

1. Become aware of the prejudicial lines that you find running through your thoughts, or appearing in your conversations. Track down the old habit-recordings which play like taped messages from your past. You may not be able to erase these tapes, but you can pull the ear plug, hit the off-switch, refuse to listen.

2. Become aware of the uses of humor to support old "my-race-is-better-than-yours" feelings. If you find yourself telling Polock, Newfie, Jewish, Chinese, Negro, Indian jokes (name your favorites), try own-

ing what you're doing then and there. Put your honest intentions into words.

3. To break free to venture trust, love, and understanding, consider:

(1) How am I stopping myself from seeing all persons, regardless of race, nationality, culture, as precious just as I am precious?

(2) How am I scaring myself from starting friendships, learning to appreciate the richness of differences, developing genuine empathy for others?

(3) How am I stuck in old prejudiced viewpoints that are unfaithful to the Jesus I want to follow daily in life?

1. Hubert Schwartzentruber, *Probe,* James Fairfield, editor, (Scottdale: Herald Press, 1972), pp. 80, 81.
2. Lowell Noble, "What's Behind Our Interracial Marriage Taboos?" *Eternity,* July 1972, p. 13.
3. *Ibid.*
4. James P. Carse, "Interracial Marriage: A Christian View," *The Christian Century,* June 14, 1967, p. 782.
5. Hans Denk, Anabaptist reformer, sixteenth century.

9

Choosing Loyalties:
The Wisdom of Conscience

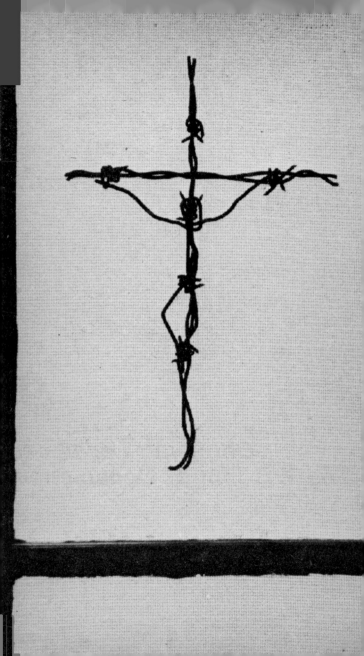

_____,
LOVE IT OR LEAVE IT!

_____

GO HOME!

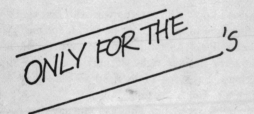

ONLY FOR THE _____'s

_____

I,_____ _____

do solemnly swear to

(say when and where)

_____

(To fill in the blanks
To sign blank-check allegiance
Is not love of country.)

"I don't know who the guy was who first said, 'My country, right or wrong,' but he said it for me," your brother quips. "As far as I'm concerned, whatever the country does is right. It may not be so smart sometimes, but none of us need to play judge and condemn it. That's treason."

You don't agree, but what can you say that he will hear? "You didn't finish the quotation," you say. "It's 'My country, right or wrong; when wrong to make it right, when right to make it just.' If you like the line, you might want to consider the whole statement."

"Look," he says, "you and I just don't know enough facts to criticize the top men. They know what they're doing. Leave the big decisions to them."

"I don't want to make their decisions for them, but I want them to know what their citizens' values are. I'm not in favor of taking advantage of little nations. I don't want to see more decisions that favor business over labor. I'm not interested in tax dodges for the rich that penalize the little guy. And, I'm not for war to improve our economy and raise our GNP."

* * *

Once upon a time, it was an accepted and appropriate thing to love one's nation above all, insist on its rights at the expense of all, and demand that it be placed above all!

That time is gone. Our world is too small. The needs about us are too vast. The possibility of closing our eyes to the hurts of others is too dangerous, too irresponsible, too tragic to envision that as any solution.

Any nationalism that insists "we must be number one" as the fundamental axiom of truth is unworthy.

(Although in America, for example, when a politician speaks on behalf of an act of legislation, it is commonly taken as the last word that America should never be anything but number one, and no price is too great to keep it number one.)

I can take pride in the creative performance of my nation. I do enjoy being a part of that able and productive thrust.

But I do not believe—nor likely do you—that maintaining the number one position of the United States at all costs is the final goal of history. I do not believe that international domination of the globe by any one nation is necessarily the will of God for His earth.

"Broad humanity exalts a nation, but narrow nationalism is a reproach to any people."

143

"Whatever they ask, that is what you have to do," you say to your son. "I mean the government's the government, and that's all there is to it, see?"

"Oh no," he replies. "I don't sign away my soul on a blank check for anybody, any party. Don't expect me to say, 'Here I am, I'll go anywhere, do anything, obey any order, when, what, or where!' "

So your sons say you give automatic knee-jerk agreement to anything the government says. He wants to think for himself, choose for himself, decide on the basis of his own conscience. "You just can't do that," you tell him. "If everyone is free to make his own decisions on what's moral and what isn't, where will we end up?"

"Look," he says, "I'm me. A person. Not a blank check. And I'm responsible for my choices. The My Lai trials showed that. And I'm going to make my decisions by my own conscience, understand?"

Yes, you're beginning to. "And," you grudgingly admit, "the boy's making a lot of sense." But then he should; he's your son.

* * *

It is no act of love to say, "You love my country just as I love my country or you leave my country."

It is not love of country to say, "My country, right or wrong." Love begins when we say, "My country, right or wrong; where wrong, to make it right; where right, to make it merciful and just."

"Righteousness exalteth a nation: but sin is a re-proach to any people (Proverbs 14:34, *KJV*).

It is not love of country to say, "I pledge allegiance, total allegiance to my nation." Blind patriotism is no service to any country. Love begins when we pledge allegiance to truth, to justice, to compassion, to concern for brothers, neighbors, for the good of all men both within and without our country's borders.

To love one's country is to care enough to challenge it with worthy goals and call it to the highest good for all.

"Right goals exalt a nation, but lack of vision is a reproach to any people."

To love one's country is to be concerned enough to confront it with honesty and call it to seek after truth.

"Open honesty exalts a nation, but falsehood and deception are a reproach to any people."

To love one's country is to be committed enough to see the needs for change, to call for change, to pray for change, to work for change.

"Willing repentance exalts a nation, but stubborn blindness is a reproach to any people."

Either we love it—by caring, challenging, confronting, and changing—or we lose it. It's not love it and let it alone, or leave. It's love it, change it, or lose it.

* * *

"I'm never opening my mouth at work on how I feel about any political issues, or race troubles, or any of that," you tell your wife. "That bunch of bluenosed conservatives would pick me clean like a flock of vultures."

"You're going to just stay mum, eh?" she asks.

"Yeah, buy me a turtleneck; I'm keeping my head in."

"But what does it do to you inside to keep your honest feelings hidden?" your wife asks.

"I don't know," you say. "It does make me look like a different man than I really am. I've got to do better than that. I want to be able to put what I really feel on the line—and still stay in touch with the guys. Maybe that's the secret."

No man is disloyal to his country's highest good when he chooses to act responsibly, think responsibly, choose responsibly on the basis of his own conscience. A conscience can be wrong, of course. But to respect it, examine it, exercise it, and obey it is the only way to be truly human, or to be the responsible human God intends us to be—as shown in Jesus.

* * *

Following the conscience is no longer automatically suspect. Once it was thought to make a man an intolerable misfit, out of step with the rank and file, and since different, someone to be feared.

Fortunately, this is changing. We are coming to recognize that conscience is not a faculty to be feared but a human quality to be prized and valued.

Without conscientious wisdom, human beings become inhuman. Persons become unquestioning robots. And human community becomes a mass of pliable and pitiable puppets manipulated by the strings of any chance chain of command.

With a "conscientious wisdom," women and men become persons of integrity, sensitive to values, committed to truth.

"Conscientious wisdom" is the necessary quality. It is a conscience open to and committed to truth—a conscience informed by obedience to this knowledge.

It must be a "conscientious wisdom"—not blind obedience to conscience. A conscience unexamined, unexplored, untested by truth can be a dangerous, even a deadly guide. No man will kill you with less compunction than a man who kills in obedience to his conscience. But a "conscientious wisdom" is a conscience open to, instructed by, and committed to the highest truth man has found in all that is available to him.

True, there are risks to following conscience. But more crimes have been committed in the name of duty and obedience to authority than in the name of conscience.

"Conscientious wisdom" is a love of truth. It is obedience to truth. It is a willingness to examine and test all truth, to sift from the good the better, from the better the best, from the best the ultimate.

"Conscientious wisdom" is a kind of courage. It is the courage to be a person. Courage to believe in values. Courage to see meaning in life. Courage to act with purpose. Courage to conform one's loyalties to one's true scale of priorities.

"Conscientious wisdom" always demands courage because following the conscience is a vulnerable act. It exposes a woman or a man to ridicule, to anger, to public rejection, to shame, to suffering, even to violence.

(Consider Martin Luther King, a man who acted in conscience, a man who died for conscience' sake. Three years before his death I heard him say to a network newscaster, "If I choose to go on living by my conscience, I may survive at the most for five more years. I could compromise my conscience and perhaps live to be eighty. Either way I die. The one way I would simply postpone my burial.")

"Conscientious wisdom" may be an act of faith. The faith that your decision is the most responsible choice open to you. The faith that choosing the right thing is the best thing even though the cost seems staggering. The faith that time will vindicate the rightness of your act even though friends may condemn you now.

* * *

"That boy will be a CO only over my dead body," your husband says.

He's beginning to shout at you, and you're only reporting what your son's letter said.

"No son of mine is going to be a—conscientious objector. If he doesn't want to volunteer, okay. But to declare himself a CO is senseless."

"It's his decision, not yours," you say.

"So you're supporting the kid's yellow ideas," your husband snaps. "Or are they pink?"

All kinds of words rush to your tongue in defense of your son. You bite them back; your son doesn't need your protection. Not against his own father. All he needs is an honest—and caring—mother, and you can be both without letting this divide your marriage. "Dear, listen," you say. "I don't want this or anything else to come between us, understand?"

He nods.

"Let's stick to our own decisions, and let our son make his. Neither of us agree with all the choices he makes. We see this one from different sides, but that's okay."

"You want him to go yellow?" your husband asks.

"No, I want him to be a man, who's free to choose his own values and live them."

It's not only your son's right, but it's his responsibility to make decisions by his own conscience. Love is not based on agreement. Loyalty to your son doesn't depend on his conforming to your expectations. Love accepts the other when disagreements and differences are real, even painful. Love can afford to disagree, because it stays in touch. There are times when God couldn't agree with you less. And still He loves.

* * *

If a war were declared unjust, by international opinion, by your religious principles, by other men of careful thought . . . would you fight in it?

Would you fight in a war which you consider an unjust war, an unjustifiable war, an immoral war? For example. If you had been a twenty-year-old male citizen of Germany in 1940, would you have obeyed orders to machine gun Jewish mothers, daughters, and babies into a muddy trench grave? Or would you have fought in the Rhineland in unquestioning obedience if you saw your regime committing the mass murder of the Jewish race?

Would you really refuse to fight in an unjust war? If so, how do you go about determining whether the war is or is not unjust?

You can't use the twenty-twenty vision of historical hindsight. You won't likely have access to international opinion, in order to shape your own in a time of national crisis.

When you come right down to it, the responsibility rests on you. On your conscience. On your best insight, your convictions, your principles, your sense of truth. You must be either a conscientious supporter, or a conscientious objector to a particular war, or to all war.

How, then, do men of good conscience go about deciding if a war is justifiable or not?

The first option: A Blank-Check Decision. Any war that my government declares or enters, I must support, and anything my government asks I'm responsible to obey.

We are responsible to obey our government. But to obey it responsibly is one thing. To follow it blindly is another. To give the state a blank check, "I'll go anywhere, do anything to anyone in obedience to any command," is to cease being a moral being—a human being.

If you accept any justification for war, you will fight in any war—just or unjust, legal or criminal.

No, the blind obedience of a blank-check attitude just won't do for men of conscience.

A second option: The Holy War. Any war that

defends our American way of life is holy, right, and good.

Is our American way of life good simply because it is American? Of course not. To give everything for one's country, simply because it is one's country, is absolute worship. That's nationalism become a religion. Patriotism turned into idolatry. It denies that there is a God in heaven whose truth is eternal and whose kingdom is above all. Such idolatry is neither moral nor rational.

Sometimes this argument is stated, "Any war that defends our Christian nation, or Christendom against communism, or Christians against paganism is automatically right." Muslims, Marxists, Maoists, and Christians have gone to battle to advance their causes. But to justify a war as a "Christian crusade" is like talking of dry wetness or hot coldness. Jesus Christ never sanctioned war, never approved violence. His every word and action repudiated man's way of hate, murder, violence, and self-defense. He laid down His life for the sake of others. He did not take the sword even in self-defense.

Self-defense is no Christian virtue. If the survival of our culture, or our own survival is our sole remaining purpose, we are not Christian. Survival is not a Christian virtue. Life is not to be maintained by any means. The ends do not justify the means.

The third option: A Just War. Through the centuries, men have agonized over the decisions of how certain acts of violence or warfare may be justified. When a conflict qualifies by certain criteria as justifiable, it has been called "a just war." (Just is short for justifiable. No war can be truly considered "just" to all involved.)

The Greeks originated the concept. "A just war" was any war declared by the Greeks against the non-Greeks, the Barbarians. The Romans added the criteria that such a war must be (1) fought by soldiers, not civilians and (2) that it must be fought with just means for just causes. Christians (after Constantine baptized his entire army into the church in the year 300) adapted those criteria for themselves.

Today our standards for a just war have been set forth in our individual national constitutions, sharpened by the Geneva Conventions on warfare, and canonized in the creeds of most major Christian denominations.

All agree on four major issues:

A just war must be (1) declared by a just authority, (2) fought for the one justifiable cause of establishing an orderly and just peace, (3) fought with justifiable proportionality between the amount of harm done and the benefits hoped for, and (4) fought by a just means, respecting noncombatants, and refusing inhumane weapons.

Do thoughtful men—Christian men—apply these principles when they are called up to fight? The record is not too good. When wars are being waged by other nations, men of conscience are seldom hesitant to apply the criteria. But when our own nation is involved, we lose both objectivity and motivation to think in clear moral terms.

If we are going to be human beings, to be responsible men, or what is more, to be Christian men, the alternatives are (1) either we can endure the agony

152

of deciding on the justice or injustice of war, or (2) we can reject war.

For the first two hundred years of the Christian faith, Christ's followers, like their Master, renounced the sword, rejected war and died refusing violence even in self-defense. By the year 400, Augustine was approving a "just war"; by the year 1000 "Christians" were fighting "holy" crusades; and by the twentieth century churches and Christians were accepting violence, as long as it served to stop the Nazis, the Fascists, the communists. During the two World Wars, bishops blessed bayonets and bazookas on both sides.

History testifies to the difficulty of making this decision. Christian thinker John Howard Yoder asks, "Did any Christians [who held to a 'just war' doctrine] ever conclude, after their government had committed itself to war that the cause was unjustified and/or the means used were inappropriate and that therefore they should not serve? Such cases [prior to Vietnam] are few, or nonexistent."

Once war is declared, the pressures to give blanket approval usually win out over any and all moral considerations. For pragmatic, expedient reasons, we choose "to accommodate the integrity of love to the realities of life."

Christ Himself chose not to accommodate. He chose love as the final basis of action and acted consistently with that love. His associate, Peter, reports; "Indeed this is . . . your calling. For Christ suffered for you and left you a personal example, and wants you to follow in his steps. He was guilty of no sin nor of the slightest prevarication. Yet when he was in-

sulted he offered no insult in return. When he suf
fered he made no threats of revenge. He simply com
mitted his cause to the one who judges fairly" (1
Peter 2:21-23, *Phillips*).

"Yes, yes, well and good," many say in response
to all this, "but I'm not Jesus. So He was absolutely
sure of Himself, His principles, His position, His ac
tions. But I can't be. So I accommodate, and go to
war. It stands to reason. It's just good sense!"

Does it stand to reason? What about this argument
that "Christ's demands are too absolute, too narrow
too single-minded to work in an imperfect world"?

Granted, all people and all human ways of life are
imperfect. That's only another way of saying that we
humans, at our best, are only relatively right. (That
is not to say that right and wrong are relative.) It is
the honest confession that no one of us has all the
facts, all the insight, or possesses all truth.

But that is no argument against Christ's way o
nonviolence. It's the very reverse.

If our best reasons and decisions are only partially
or relatively good, then to take absolute and final ac
tions—to snuff out lives with bombs, to singe the
earth bare of people with napalm, to exterminate one
man, or a whole nation as in Vietnam—all in pursui
of some imperfect relative good is irresponsible to
Jesus Christ.

I am not attempting to prove Christ's way by
logic. I am asserting that man's logic invariably
works both ways and ultimately even human reason
betrays us.

And I am insisting that for the Christian the only
responsible way is to discover what Christ actually

154

taught, what Christ actually demanded, how Christ actually acted and reacted, and how Christ's eyewitnesses understood all that He communicated. And then, responsibility is to obey the Christ and follow Him in life.

* * *

This is a time for a call to conscience.

It is a time for a call to go out from all men who value acts of conscience to all who hope to live in all good conscience.

"Let us speak, act, and be the truth."

Nothing less is being responsible to God, to man, to our nation, to our world, to our friends or to our enemies. Obedience to conscience is the only true patriotism. Obedience to truth is the only true statesmanship.

If you choose to fight in wars you consider just, come to your decision in clear open exercise of your conscience, weighing all truth available to you. I choose to reject all war as outside the way and will of Jesus. He is, for me, the final truth.

"You shall know the truth, and the truth shall make you free." Favorite words of Jesus! But the whole word is, "If you are faithful to what I have said, you are truly my disciples. And you will know the truth and the truth will set you free!" (John 8:31,32, *Phillips*).

As Jesus put it—to be responsible to all the truth available to us, to be responsible to God the ultimate Judge of truth, to be responsible to the Christ who demonstrated truth in life in the most perfect way

155

known in the history of man—this is the freedom of conscientious wisdom, the freedom of truth.

For Further Discussion

1. Examine the four classic alternatives for the Christian conscience and participation in warfare.

(1) The blank-check approach. Whatever my government asks, I must do. The Bible commands obedience. I am not morally responsible for any acts done when under orders. (Nuremberg, Tokyo, the My Lai trials all say otherwise.)

(2) The holy-war stance. Any war that defends a Christian nation or Christendom against communism is a crusade for liberty, justice, and righteousness. (Christians believed this in the Middle Ages. It has had no continuing support by any Christian group except in times of great national stress.)

(3) The just-war conviction. A war can be justified if (a) declared by just authority, (b) fought to bring a just and orderly peace, (c) fought with clear proportionality between amount of harm and benefits hoped for, (d) fought by just means, by combatants only, without inhumane weapons.

(4) Nonviolent love. War only creates the conditions for the following wars. Violence breeds new and more vicious violent reprisals. Someone must break the cycle. Jesus called His followers to accept this challenge unconditionally. (Refusing to participate in violence is risky. There is no guarantee of either survival or success.)

Peacemaking is
care-fronting,
truthing it,
owning responsibility,
growing,
trusting,
forgiving,
accepting,
canceling demands,
dropping blame,
forgetting prejudice,
acting in loving
reconciling ways.

Making peace is the
Jesus way.

CASE ONE: A personal profile. Nonfiction fiction. He was born into a talented, highly competitive family: brilliant father; creative mother; winning sisters; strong, successful brothers.

But he? He looked ordinary, performed average, achieved the usual, won no attention or recognition.

In another family he might have accepted his place as an average, normal, ordinary-contributing Mr. Everybody. But here—impossible.

There were his father's high expectations to deal with, not to mention his brother-sister pressures.

College? "Yes," said dad.

"No," said son.

He tried a job, business entanglements, financial responsibilities, serious courtship—all as ways of escape.

"No, no, no," said dad.

Finally he played the angry trump card. Quick marriage by elopement. He settled down to his chosen life. Forgot his family. But no satisfaction. Now that

160

he had what he had wanted, he discovered it wasn't what he wanted after all. And all the old drives to achieve, to win recognition, awoke within him.

Business success? Blind alley. Social prominence? No admission. That left him one outlet. In his church. He poured himself into it. Education was missing, so he used piety.

Piety was the master stroke. Pious activity could win respect and acclaim. Pious concerns shared as prayer requests could eliminate competitors. Conspicuous good works, done with obvious humility, could collect recognition.

Then, just as he was achieving it all, it began to slip through his fingers. So he drove stakes, defensively. This was followed by multiplying convictions, increasing conservatism, dogmatism. Then threatening rifts, schism between those valiant for the truth.

Charges. Accusations. Bitterness.

Did no one understand his battle?

Yes, yes they did. Too well.

And no one approached him? No one helped him see his own conflicts projected on others? No one cared enough to reach out with the attention, the affection, the acceptance early enough while it could still be heard?

Did no one care?

* * *

Peacemaking begins in hearing another's deep hurts.

It's much easier to avoid making contact with another's pain. All that's necessary is to quickly give advice. Tell him what to do with his troubles. Tell him where to go with his complaints. Get him off your back, out of your hair.

It's so much easier to tell another what to do about his hurts than to stand with him in his pain.

Peacemaking is first being truly present with another.

* * *

CASE TWO: He was born into a family of no wealth, no reputation, no respected position in their community. Nobodies.

His brothers and sisters—underachievers. Dropouts at grade eight or nine.

His father worked—several months out of the year.

His mother struggled to keep body and soul together by dishing out what little they had, stitching up what threads they almost no longer had, and, in general, working enough for two people.

Was it anger over his parents' negligent carelessness, their voluntary poverty? Was it humiliation from his peer group's patronizing smiles? Was it sheer frustration from his own deprived way of life? Whatever—or whichever—the reason, he was fired with a new strain of family traits.

He slugged his way through high school, making the highest grades but not becoming valedictorian (not well-rounded enough, you know; besides, you know his family). Somehow he held two jobs—one after school, one weekends. Then he broke into a small business of his own.

He had difficulties socially—seldom with the girl, almost always with the parents.

Then marriage. Financial success. Business prominence. Community recognition by people who saw him as the man he had become.

But among his old friends and in his church? There he was still the boy from that family, who grew up in that house, on that street.

So he began to press at a few points which were open to challenge—in his church. Others who shared his feelings of dissatisfaction gathered around him. Tensions grew. Rumors began to flow and float—quietly at first. Then accusations broke into the open. Old sneers at his family surfaced and circulated again.

New issues emerged.

Did no one understand? Truth was not on trial, love was. It was not a conservative-liberal conflict, or even the new versus the old. It was the "ins" against the "outs." The establishment versus the outsider, the intruder.

Did no one come to give the honest acceptance, recognition, and love needed or deserved? Was no one willing to see him for what he wanted to be, for what he had worked to become, for what he now was?

Did no one care?

* * *

Peacemaking proceeds by letting the past pass. And being present with another in the here and now.

Finish the past by dropping old demands, cancel-

163

ing old criticisms and prejudices. Accept the woman or man who is with you now.

We are all free to change, free to be new, now. Free to become who we can be. Change to new life is the natural order of things when God is at work among us. We need to go with—to flow with—His stream of life-changing growth.

* * *

CASE THREE: He was Mr. Average Citizen. Average home. Average education. Average wealth. Normal. Usual. Run-of-the-mill. Not that he was Mr. Nobody. He was Mr. Everybody.

But now and again he grew dissatisfied. Not that he consciously decided in those times, "I'm gonna throw my weight around a little." No, it was just that he had to lean the weight of his frustrations somewhere.

So he'd find himself agitating a little, criticizing a bit—"sharing concern" it is sometimes called. But doing it in hidden, covert ways.

He could apply a little pressure to get something changed just to make his presence felt too.

He could point out some problem or oversight, find some fault to rub with salt—to show that even he knew better than that and to let those on top hear from the rest of humanity.

He could quote a few appropriate criticisms when frustrations could easily be brought out into the open. Then step out, leaving others to handle them.

He could anonymously stir the troubled waters that lie beneath the surface of any group. Not with open malice, mind you, but out of the deep frustration of being a taken-for-granted bit of the social backwaters.

And in his church, where the social machine all too often runs with so little lubrication of love, his refusing to be a smoothly meshing cog in the machine generated friction—with both heat and wear.

Did no one hear? No one care? No one understand?

* * *

Wanted:
Peacemakers.
Caring-confronting people who dare to be present where people are hurting, who are willing to help finish the old business of the past and foster the freedom of persons to be who they are becoming here and now.

Life can begin again. Now. Peacemaking is believing it's not too late to start all over again. Now. Peacemaking is knowing we don't need to turn time back to find a new beginning. Now is the time.

If we are stuck, stopped in our tracks and waiting for circumstances to change before we begin appreciating life, anticipating joy with our pain, and experiencing the richness of what is, then we are stopping ourselves. We are keeping ourselves stuck. We are riding the brakes.

We can quit, when we choose. We can look for new beginnings. We can start over. Not from some past beginning, but now. We may not be able to take

165

it from the top, but we can take it from here and now, and get on with living.

* * *

"Happy are the peacemakers," Jesus once said, "because they are called God's sons."

Yes. They are. They are people who recognize the God of peace as their Father, the Prince of Peace as their leader, and the way of peacemaking as the only Christlike way of life.

Does that make them a bunch of meek, spineless, "tut-tut" murmurers who go about "now, nowing" everything?

No. They're peacemakers. They're willing to risk stepping into moments of conflict to do curative peace work, to heal torn relationships, and even do a bit of surgery where needed.

And they're also concerned about preventive peacemaking. They look for building hostilities—and help to relieve them while they're still forming, before they reach the explosive stage.

How do they do this preventive peacemaking?

By following the way of Jesus. In these specifics:

First, they judge a man, not by what he's been or what he's done, but by what he is now. If a man opens himself to Jesus as Lord, a new thing begins. Jesus-people (peacemakers) look to see what that new thing is and what form it is taking.

As the Bible puts it: "The very spring of our actions is the love of Christ. . . . This means that our knowledge of men can no longer be based on their outward lives (indeed, even though we knew Christ as a man we do not know him like that any longer). For if a man is in Christ he becomes a new person altogether—the past is finished and gone, everything has become fresh and new" (2 Corinthians 5:14,16,17, *Phillips*).

Peacemakers believe "the past is finished and gone." They live it that way.

Secondly, they look for strengths in others and encourage them. They sense where there are gifts and talents lying dormant or ignored and affirm them in others.

As the Bible says: "For just as you have many members in one physical body and those members differ in their functions, so we, though many in number, compose one body in Christ and are all members of one another.

"Let us have no imitation Christian love. Let us have a genuine break with evil and a real devotion to good. Let us have real warm affection for one another as between brothers, and a willingness to let the other man have the credit" (Romans 12:4,5,9,10, *Phillips*).

Look for opportunities of affirming, of encouraging, of helping release others to become all they can be in Christ.

Love is the important thing, not brilliant insight into persons and personalities.

Honesty is the indispensable thing, not attempting to avoid and gloss over the difficulty with a glaze of sweetness.

Love with honesty, caring with confronting, truthing it in love—these are the keys.

Concern for mutual fulfillment, self-discovery, opportunity for service and meaningful work is the real goal.

* * *

"I say let's drop him," Joe tosses the line over his shoulder as he weaves through freeway traffic. He's talking about the fifth guy in your car pool—Mike, the pain in everybody's work week. "When he gets back from vacation we'll just tell him to make other plans, okay?"

Sounds great to you. Mike is always late, morning and evening, forever imposing on the rest of you—borrowing money, holding you up with, "Stop at the corner, it'll only take a minute." He's just hard to take—tactless comments, corny jokes.

"Good riddance," you say. "Who's going to give him the axe?" Everybody's silent. Then it hits you. "You know? We've all been bugged at Mike for almost a year. Yet none of us has leveled with him. I've never told him how I feel. We all act like his imposing on us is A-OK. What if we give him the truth for a change."

"Huh-uh!" Joes says. "You can't change that bad mouth."

"No, but we can give him the benefit of a little honesty. That's what I'd want. Besides, he's not all bad."

Before you cut a guy off, and then avoid him forever after, consider caring enough to confront him with what you feel. True—you won't change him overnight. But you can negotiate new ways of getting along. You can work out some ground rules that respect everyone's rights and wants.

* * *

Peacemaking love works out the mathematics of justice.

Peacemaking love looks after each person's welfare and concerns.

Peacemaking love sees each person as precious simply because they are.

Love. The word falls short when we attempt to put all this freight within it. No one word is sufficient to state all that we mean. With one exception.

What? What is it? No one word is sufficient to describe it. It is seen perfectly in one man, in one life, in one person.

Jesus.

Substitute the name "Jesus" for Paul's word "love" in his description of this just, caring concern and things come clear.

What no single word is able to contain, one single life is able to embody and demonstrate.

"Jesus was patient, kind, never jealous, boastful or arrogant. He did not act unbecomingly, did not first seek His own interests, was not touchy, did not keep account of wrongs suffered, nor gloat over the hardships of others. His greatest joy was seeing truth come to life. He accepted all that people said or did to Him, trusted all who approached Him, believed the best for all who despaired. He set no limits for what He could endure. His concern, respect, and compassion could outlast anything."

That fleshes out the word "love." St. Paul had an unusual word available to him to sum all this meaning into verbal shorthand. "Agape" is the word in the Greek language which he used.

"Agape" has been defined as "self-sacrificial love," or "disinterested love," or "self-giving love," or "unconditional-concerned-respect," or "neighbor-regarding-love." Any attempt at expressing this love in words falls back on action words. That's where our Western languages and Western ways of thinking shortchange us. For us, love is largely a matter of feelings, attitudes, and emotional responses.

But the Jesus-style-of-love is something you do to others. It's a caring way of responding to people as persons of value. It's a confronting way of relating to people as individuals of infinite worth in God's sight, and therefore in your own.

Jesus valued the needs of the neighbor above all else. For Him, concern for others is the supreme value, the one thing of infinite worth. Any discussion of "infinite worth" and "infinite values" sounds like a lot of classy talk unless it is spelled out in specifics.

To be specific, to say Christlike love is infinitely superior in value to human knowledge is to say, No gain in human knowledge is worth even the smallest loss of neighbor-love. Or to say Christlike love is infinitely superior to any human achievements is to say, no amount of increase in human achievement and success is worth even the smallest decrease in Christ-like love.

The Jesus way of love-in-actions-of-ultimate-concern-for-others is the one course of action which is of infinite value.

The Jesus way of loving-deeds is a life-style of living *for*, unshakably *for*, unconditionally *for*, unreservedly *for* the highest good *for* others. (Not in servile obedience to human whims, but in concerned commitment to the highest good for others.)

Persons matter most.

Those who live in the Jesus-way—call it love if you will—seek the highest good they can find (God's kingly rule) and share it in acted-out deeds of loving service, concern, respect, and even self-sacrifice.

People matter most.

They act in love, not because it is the safe thing to do. (It doesn't guarantee either success or survival.) Nor because it is the brilliant thing to do. (It seldom is the clever strategy, or the pragmatic route of common sense.) They act in love because it is the Jesus thing to do, the Jesus way to live, the Jesus kind of loving.

And since He alone has triumphed in the one permanent victory of all time—love acted out on a cross —His way is the only way that is certain to triumph totally, finally, ultimately, eternally.

So, for those who have come to accept this Jesus as supreme commander of creation, and to regard His words and His ways as the final authority on life and living, for such people this strange quality of love keeps cropping out.

At unusual times, in unexpected ways, with unexplainable strength, this undefinable "something" appears.

It's the Jesus way of living, flawlessly demonstrated in the Jesus of the New Testament, and made possible today by the Jesus strength-to-love which Christians call the Holy Spirit.

It's possible.

It's happening.

It's now—for those who know Him now and follow Him daily in life.

For Further Thought

1. If conflict is natural, neutral, and potentially creative, as well as possibly destructive, how can Christians best fulfill their roles as peacemakers?

(1) By avoiding conflict?

(2) By denouncing conflict?

(3) Or by becoming creative persons who choose the love-fight and break through barriers by caring-confronting persistence?

2. If conflict can become a creative force for honest intimacy, how do we work at differences?

(1) Discarding hidden strategies so that varied views and concealed disagreements can be exposed?

(2) Increasing both trust and risk so that hidden factors can be shared and fearful people can experiment with openness?

(3) Initiating love-truth, care-confront conversations where individuality can be expressed and then unity chosen and celebrated?

3. Since love is *the way* to perceive you as well as me, I want to love you enough to tell you the truth, and be truthful enough to demonstrate my love. To care-front. To truth it with you. To experience the love-fight.

The Author

David Augsburger, Nancy, his wife, and their two daughters, Deborah and Judith, live at Elkhart, Indiana, where David teaches at the Associated Mennonite Biblical Seminaries.

Before moving to Elkhart he taught pastoral psychology and counseling at Northern Baptist Theological Seminary, Oak Brook, Illinois.

He completed his doctoral studies in pastoral psychotherapy and family therapy at the School of Theology at Claremont in Claremont, California.

Born in Delphos, Ohio, David received his B.A. degree from Eastern Mennonite College and his B.D. degree from Eastern Mennonite Seminary. Both are located in Harrisonburg, Virginia.

The Augsburgers served two pastorates from 1960 to 1970. From 1966 through 1974 he was speaker for the Mennonite Church's radio release, *The Mennonite Hour.*

In 1971· he received the Gabriel Award for CHOICE, a daily radio 5-minute broadcast for men. He has scripted many radio spots, special seasonal broadcasts, and Family Life TV spots.

He is author of eight books, including: *Cherishable: Love and Marriage, A Risk Worth Taking, Communicating Good News, Seventy Times Seven, Man Uptight,* and *Be All You Can Be.*